Helping Your Children Feel Good about Themselves

Helping Your Children Feel Good about Themselves

A Guide to Building Self-Esteem in the Christian Family

KENNETH A. ERICKSON

Augsburg
MINNEAPOLIS

HELPING YOUR CHILDREN FEEL GOOD ABOUT THEMSELVES
A Guide to Building Self-Esteem in the Christian Family

Scripture quotations unless otherwise noted are from the New Revised Standard Version Bible, copyright © 1989 by the Division of Christian Education of the National Council of the Churches of Christ in the USA and used by permission.

Scripture quotations noted TEV are from the *Good News Bible*—Old Testament: copyright © 1976 by the American Bible Society; New Testament: copyright © 1966, 1971, 1976 by the American Bible Society. Used by permission.

Scripture quotations noted RSV are from the Revised Standard Version of the Bible, copyright © 1946, 1952, 1971 by the Division of Christian Education of the National Council of the Churches of Christ in the USA. Used by permission.

Scripture quotations noted NEB are from *The New English Bible*, copyright © 1961, 1970 by the Delegates of the Oxford University Press and the Syndics of the Cambridge University Press. Reprinted by permission.

Cartoons copyright © 1992 Bill Keane, Inc. Distributed by Cowles Syndicate, Inc. Reprinted with special permission of King Features Syndicate.

"Lord, If I Am Unique" copyright © Herb Brokering. Used by permission.

Cover design by Cindy Cobb Olson
Interior design by Ann Elliot Artz

Library of Congress Cataloging-in-Publication Data

Erickson, Kenneth A.
   Helping your children feel good about themselves : a guide to
building self-esteem in the Christian family / Kenneth A. Erickson
      p. cm.
   Includes bibliographical references.
   ISBN 0-8066-2729-8 :
   1. Self-esteem in children.   2. Child rearing—Religious aspects—
Christianity.   3. Parenting—Religious aspects—Christianity.
4. Family—Religious life. I. Title.
BF723.S3E75   1994
248.8'45—dc20   94-19798
                                            CIP

Manufactured in the U.S.A.   AF 9-2729

98   97   96   95   94   1   2   3   4   5   6   7   8   9   10

CONTENTS

Author Charlie Shedd says that before he was a parent he was confident as a young pastor in speaking to fathers and mothers about raising their offspring. His first message was titled "Some Suggestions for Parents." Then he had children of his own and he changed his talk to "Feeble Hints to Fellow Strugglers." After his children were grown, he was invited to address an audience of parents. He began, "Does anyone here have a few words of wisdom?"

We all come to the responsibility of parenthood without previous experience. When provoked, we revert to the child-raising routines our parents used on us. Sometimes these are helpful and affirming to our children and increase their self-esteem; sometimes our actions are cruel and demeaning and decrease their self-esteem. Children see each action as accepting, indifferent, or rejecting. These early feelings determine how they will see themselves throughout their lifetime.

A child's self-esteem declines between kindergarten and high school. Notice in the chart on the following page how critical the years from five to ten are. Parental attitudes and actions are also important to a child between the ages of ten and seventeen because in these years, a young person's sense of self-worth drops to an all-time low.

Percent of children who report that they possess a sense of self-esteem (National Center for Self-esteem, 1987)

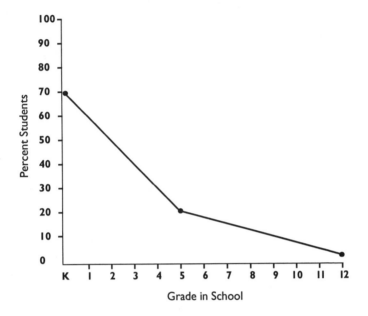

Grade in School

Psychologist James Dobson describes detrimental by-products of low self-esteem:

> The matter of personal worth is not only the concern of those who lack it. In a real sense, the health of an entire society depends on the ease with which the individual members gain personal acceptance. Thus, whenever the keys to self-esteem are seemingly out of reach for a large percentage of the people, as in twentieth-century America, then widespread "mental illness," neuroticism, hatred, alcoholism, drug abuse, violence, and social disorder will certainly occur.[1]

Parenting is tough but it is one of the most significant responsibilities adults will ever assume. Few of us have any special preparation for it. No how-to manuals accompany a child's birth certificate. We learn from our mistakes, but by the time we are more knowledgeable, our kids are grown and gone.

A recent study shows that the top interests for youth include:

Knowing how to make friends and be a friend 67%
Learning to like myself more 62%
Learning how to talk better with my parents .... 50%[2]

Did you catch that middle line, parent? *Learning to like myself more.* . . . Are you willing to accept this crucial responsibility to nourish your child's self-esteem? Are you eager to see your child's sense of self-worth blossom and grow?

The essence of *Helping Your Children Feel Good about Themselves* is drawn from twenty years of experience working with thousands of youths and their parents while I served as a teacher, counselor, principal, and school superintendent. I learned valuable truths from exemplary as well as tragic parent-child relationships. I also learned from the successes and errors of my own parents, plus the mistakes I made while my wife Lois and I raised our three children and a foster son.

The guidelines that follow can provide a lifetime of precious relationships that will bless not only your own family but those of your descendants for many years to come.

ACKNOWLEDGMENTS

Sincere appreciation goes to my wife, Lois, for her unconditional love, support, and constructive critiques throughout this writing project. My thanks also go to Norm Rohrer and Heino Heinsoo for their special assistance.

In addition I wish to recognize many friends who shared personal experiences and insights regarding the importance of self-worth. These include George Benson, Agnes Best, Harvey Blomberg, Leo Bustad, Carol Christ, Ron Coen, Marty Dasler, Dan Erlander, Ellen Gamrath, Jim Girvan, Bob Grover, Steve Grumm, Penny Guntermann, Jon Hellstedt, Howard Horner, Bob Keller, Eunice Kjaer, Lisa Livelybrooks, Ed Markwardt, Karen McIntyre, Merle Ohlsen, Peter Steinke, Neal Stixrud, Doc Streator, Jim Thiessen, Walt Vernstrom, Al White, Howard Widoff, and Zane Wilson. To each a heartfelt "Thank you!"

1

Where Self-Esteem Begins

*My view of myself when a child was
a composite picture of all my reflections
mirrored by other people . . .
particularly . . . by my mother and dad.*

—Rev. Penny Guntermann

Reflected images are powerful. I've always enjoyed visits to the hall of mirrors at a fair or circus. Children do, too. They delight in their misshapen reflections—pumpkin-shaped heads, giraffelike necks, ballooning stomachs, and bean-pole legs. Of course, we realize that these exaggerations are due to deliberate imperfections in the mirroring surface.

In the home, however, children accept as authentic those images reflected by their mom and dad. As a result, parental reflections become etched in each child's subconscious mind. Such perceptions are a powerful influence in the formation of self-concept. Once set, the mirrored self-image resists modification.

THE ROOTS OF SELF-ESTEEM

God looks at each of us, children as well as adults, as a person of infinite worth. God's love is beyond our comprehension, but knowing how much we are loved, in spite of our imperfections and faults, can be the firm foundation of our self-esteem. If we are loved so much, we figure, we must be valuable.

Teaching children the almost-unbelievable truth about God's love is one of the major tasks of parents. Through family devotions, the reading of Bible stories, conversations, and actions, parents can keep presenting this reassurance to children: God loves and accepts you now and forever, just as you are! This is one reflection, one mirror, that tells them only good news.

THE IMPORTANCE OF FAMILY DEVOTIONS

The earnest prayer of a righteous person has
great power and wonderful results.
—James 5:16b (TEV)

In our materialistic society, parents need all the help available to raise to maturity each child in their care. This help includes intercessory prayer. Uphold each child before God in daily family devotions; thank God for each family member by name. It can be comforting to a child's sense of belonging if family members join hands when praying during family devotions or saying the blessing at mealtime. Adding a little squeeze of the hand at the end can communicate love and enhance a child's self-esteem. When children are away from home, assure them of your continuing prayers in their behalf.

During family devotions, we can model positive attitudes of self-acceptance for our children. We can let them hear us pray, "Sometimes, God, I'm concerned about being 'different.' I worry what others might think of me because I'm a follower of your way. Help me to remember that it's your love, forgiveness, and acceptance that support me at all times."

Another sustaining family prayer is simple: "Regardless of what happens to me today, God, I know that I'm never second best in your eyes. I know you love me and accept me all the time. I am your beloved child."

NOTICE AND AFFIRM THE BEST

Parents play an important role in helping children learn which of their actions are beneficial and healthy, and which are destructive and unhealthy. Usually we induce the behavior from children that we recognize and respond to. Do we commend a child's noble actions or do we fume about shortcomings? Whatever behavior we make an issue of is behavior we are likely to see repeated.

As a high school principal, I learned that if I obviously overreacted when one student defaced a locker door, others wanting attention might say to themselves, "Aha! If we really want to

bug the principal, all we have to do is mess up more locker doors!"
On the other hand, if I quietly handled the problem with the student
involved, there would be no follow-up reaction from others to the
discipline.

This technique works in positive ways as well. The students
at the high school of which I was principal conducted themselves
remarkably well during a hotly contested basketball game by not
responding to the taunts of students from another school. When
I reacted with public praise and commendation, the students' sense
of self-esteem grew and their corporate behavior improved no-
ticeably. My recognition encouraged more of the positive conduct
that I had applauded.

This same principle is effective in the home. The conduct
to which parents respond is the behavior their children know will
get attention. If we react mainly to children's problems, we foster
more undesirable behavior. If we recognize and appreciate children's willingness to help with various tasks, we encourage their
eagerness to carry out other positive actions in the future.

Tyler quickly learns to repeat conduct that gets a reaction
from Mom and Dad. If they respond to negative conduct, Tyler
will repeat it. If they lose their cool every time Tyler leaves his
bicycle in the driveway, he may repeat that offense when he needs
their attention later. On the other hand, if Mom and Dad recognize
daughter Alyssa's good work in helping to clear the table after
meals, she's apt to volunteer often because of their affirmation.
Seeking to enhance a child's self-esteem by recognizing good work
can effect a significant improvement in overall behavior.

RESPONSIBILITY AND SELF-ESTEEM

*Teach a child how he should live, and he will
remember it all his life.*
—Proverbs 22:6 (TEV)

We know that our affirmations and attention to our children's positive actions help build their self-esteem, but we may
forget something else that is also helpful. The assignment of specific duties in the home is recognized as one of the most effective
ways to teach responsibility. As children see that they are able

to carry out their assigned tasks, their self-esteem improves. Child psychologists say that having responsibilities at home gives youngsters needed feelings of accomplishment, belonging, and self-respect. Unfortunately, many kids are deprived of such assignments and fail to benefit from the positive feelings of accomplishment.

To assign specific duties at home, you might make a Chore Chart for each child who is old enough to read. List tasks on the left side and write when the task is to be completed. Check-off boxes for each chore's completion may prove helpful. The major advantage of the Chore Chart is that it's both impersonal and authoritative. Placed in a conspicuous place on the refrigerator or wall, it prevents the need for constant reminders by parents as well as claims of forgetfulness by children. Regular parental recognition and appreciation for work done well and on time strengthens positive work habits and boosts a child's sense of self-worth.

TOO MUCH OF A GOOD THING

As a high school principal with final responsibility for discipline, I was often thrust into the middle of "Problem City." Wanting to help young people and parents view their troubles more positively, I posted a sign in my office that read "PROBLEMS = POSSIBILITIES = PROGRESS." I hoped that the motto would encourage both students and parents to view difficulties as challenges that can lead to personal growth.

Nathan's mom and dad went to great lengths to shield their son from any discipline in relation to his problems. Nathan was blessed with many academic, athletic, and social gifts. From his parents' viewpoint he could do no wrong. Whenever Nathan did have a problem at school, his parents tried to protect him from the consequences of his misdeeds. They would blame friends, teachers, or the school for his difficulties.

A graphic example of parental overprotection occurred when Nathan stole a car. To absolve his son of the offense, Nathan's father arranged to buy the car with an unclear date of sale. The dad then claimed that Nathan, knowing his father was planning to purchase the vehicle, had made the understandable mistake of picking up the car too soon. By this ploy, Nathan was cleared of the serious charge of grand theft auto.

Later I had to place specific limits on Nathan's campus activities. I explained to the family that if he violated the rules outlined we would have to expel him from school. Yet why should Nathan believe that any limits really applied to him? Before long he had ignored the boundaries established and found himself expelled. Since Nathan was a senior and needed to graduate, I arranged for him to complete two required courses elsewhere.

I was pleased with Nathan's reaction when he heard what his options were. He realized that I had cared enough for him to demonstrate that there really were limits in life. We respected each other and became friends. He got a job working afternoons at a service station. I would often drive to his place of work and have my car serviced.

I'm convinced that Nathan's consistent misdeeds were a cry for help. For years he was bewildered, wondering, "What do I have to do, Mom and Dad, to really get your attention? Don't you care enough about me to set some limits?" He probably sensed that his parents were more concerned about their reputation than about what was best for their son. As a result, Nathan was searching for someone who would say "No" and then care enough to make it stick. Parents who bail their children out of each difficulty do them no service. They deny them the stability associated with loving limits, deprive them of some of life's best learning experiences, and damage their children's self-esteem.

INFLUENCES FROM THE PAST

"Children are living messages we send to a time we'll never see," wrote Neil Postman. Good parenting gets them to their destination as healthy and happy adults.

The lasting effects of both positive and negative parenting are endless. They flow forward from generation to generation. Unless we make conscious efforts to improve on some of the practices we experienced as children, we tend to raise our sons and daughters as we were raised.

Intergenerational parenting practices are everyday realities. While some parents praise, others demean their child's self-image by lashing out with bruising words. Battered by such treatment, many young people pledge never to use words as weapons against their own children. Yet years later, as frustrated parents, they find themselves automatically using the same abrasive comments. In this way the curse of child humiliation is passed from generation to generation. Only continual vigilance and prayers for divine guidance can change the patterns of intergenerational parenting practices.

Psychologist Paul Tournier identifies one reason parents may act in domineering ways toward a child. He describes a withdrawn youngster who "has been crushed by the authoritarian discipline of his father who is unconsciously getting vengeance for the authority from which he suffered in his childhood."[1]

On a television talk show a member of the audience asked, "How can I change my parenting practices to do better than my mom and dad?"

The host replied, "Normally, we raise our children the way we were raised. We don't realize that if we were always yelled at as a child, and even if it hurt very much, the thing we really know how to do well with our own children is to yell. Such learned reactions become habits that are difficult to break, particularly in the heat of a parent-child conflict."

Those of us who experienced negative parenting as children have two choices. We can perpetuate damaging relationships by raising our children as we were raised. Or, with God's help, we can overcome our inherited negative habit patterns. In doing this we not only improve how our children are nurtured but we also positively influence how they will raise *their* children.

TEN WAYS TO INCREASE A CHILD'S SELF-ESTEEM

1. Keep reminding your children how much God loves them. God accepts each one of them as a beloved child, never forgets any child, and is always with each child. Ask God for the ability to accept each of your children with a love patterned after the generous, unconditional, dependable divine love.

2. Treat children as if they already are what you want them to become. Youngsters react to such trust by striving to live up to parental expectations. This enhances their self-confidence.

"They look so sweet and peaceful when
they're asleep. You wonder how they could
ever yell at us during the day."

3. Establish caring limits and stick to them. At times young-sters will complain and test the limits to see if you really care what they do, but inwardly they appreciate adults who are consistent, respectful, and firm.

4. Work to modify inherited negative parenting practices. This is not easy to do. Pray for patience whenever you are inclined to react in harmful ways to a child's irritating goofs and oversights.

5. Drop your concerns and problems when you come home and focus on your children. When they arrive home from work, parents may still be under the stress of job-related problems. Identify a receptacle near the door where you can mentally stuff the cares of the day before meeting your family.

6. Promptly admit your mistakes and omissions. By asking forgiveness of a family member you have hurt, you'll endow each child's future with positive examples of requesting and accepting forgiveness.

7. Spare your children the duplicitous love that says, "I'll love you if you do exactly as I say." Love that has strings attached is phony. It frustrates the child, who worries, "If I make more mistakes, will my parents be able to love me?"

8. If parent-child tensions still persist at the end of a day's activities, try to resolve them at bedtime. Seek outside help (from a pastor or counselor, for example) if they persist.

9. Pray *with* your children as well as *for* them.

10. At bedtime, comment on some special strength or positive act of each child. Such thoughts tend to remain in the child's subconscious all night.

INSIGHTS FOR PARENTS

I. The younger a child is when influenced by positive or negative parental reactions, the deeper and more lasting the impact on that child's self-image.

2. "Children are like wet cement. Whatever falls on them makes an impression."—Haim Ginott

3. No competent coach would teach tennis simply by emphasizing everything not to do. It's equally absurd for parents to focus all their attention on what a child does wrong.

4. Your children normally will value themselves as they are valued.

5. "Children have a way of becoming what you encourage them to be—not what you nag them to be."—Scudder Parker

6. If parents decide regularly to affirm an insecure child, they will be rewarded by that child's slow but steady growth toward becoming more self-confident and caring.

7. Children normally act like the persons they conceive themselves to be, a synthesis of all the reflections that significant others mirror to them.

8. Whenever possible, avoid making a big issue out of a child's improper behavior. If you must attend to it, talk with the child in a calm and reasonable manner.

9. Establish clear caring limits and use them when a child's behavior is obviously out of line. Say to the child, "I love you too much to let you act like that."

10. Our parenting examples to our children and grand-children may rank as our greatest accomplishments or most distressing failures. More than we ever realize, parents affect eternity.

THINGS TO DO

Try the activities in these "Things to Do" sections throughout this book with your spouse or in a parents' group. You may wish to invite parents from several families to meet as a discussion group in your home. You or your spouse could be the discussion leader for the first session or two. Suggest that participants agree to three sessions, after which they can decide whether to continue meeting.

If the first discussions prove helpful, invite a different parent to choose another chapter of this book and serve as discussion leader for one or more meetings. Encourage the parents to develop questions prompted by the activities suggestions at the end of each chapter. Continue such discussions as long as the meetings prove beneficial.

Here are some activities related to chapter 1:

A. Visualize each of your children as an adult. Write down five adjectives that you imagine your grown-up children will use to best describe their childhood relationships with you.

B. Below your original list, add several additional adjectives that you would like to see added to your list above.

C. Share your wish list with other parents. As a group, discuss specific parenting activities you believe would cultivate the increasingly positive relationships desired.

2

What We Do Has Lasting Effects

Ignorance . . . excuses no man.

—John Selden

Each year approximately two million teenagers leave the warmth and security of their homes for the uncertainties of life on the street. What makes living in some cardboard box or under a bridge with other runaways preferable to the security of life with parents? Why do kids accept bad food, dirty clothing, and the risk of contracting AIDS as the price of escaping their home situation?

Few parents intentionally neglect or abuse children. Yet when exhausted, frustrated, or overwhelmed, even a well-intentioned mother or father may lose control and bruise a child emotionally with thoughtless words or rash actions.

Children, like mirrors, reflect back the love they are given. They are more likely to be reservoirs full of affection when affection is provided by the parents. Even infants can sense whether they are treasured, tolerated, or unwanted. It is thought-provoking to realize that by the time a child is three years old, parents may have done half of all they can do toward shaping the child's character. If you spend much time away from home during your child's early years, be extremely careful in the selection of those who will care for and influence your child. Caregivers are a significant force in the formation of the youngster's lifelong characteristics.

A sense of self-esteem is a child's most fragile attribute. It can be shattered by a small incident. Building it back requires monumental effort and skill. A father with a sharp, critical attitude toward his children cannot expect to escape similar feelings from them in return. A child might hide contempt for a parent out of fear for many years, but it is likely to surface in adolescence.

Increasing numbers of young people suffering from inadequate self-esteem are contributing to a dramatic rise in antisocial behavior. A speaker at a conference on youth stated that:

- Every seven minutes, a youth is arrested for a drug offense.
- Every sixty-seven seconds, some teenage girl has a baby.
- Every twenty-six seconds, a child runs away from home.

Youngsters deprived of attention will seek to be noticed by almost anyone, regardless of personal cost or family distress. From the day of birth, every boy and girl needs an uninterrupted supply of parental attention and love.

THE LAKE WOEBEGON FANTASY

Many moms and dads cannot accept the fact that *their* child may be below average. They embrace the Lake Woebegon fantasy made popular by radio personality Garrison Keillor, who describes his make-believe community as a place where "all the men are strong, all the women good-looking, and all the children above average."

Most young people are nonaverage in talents, including athletic, artistic, and scholastic ability. Only a few are at the golden mean. Imagine lining up all ten-year-old girls from the shortest to the tallest. Then do the same with all ten-year-old boys. The average height in both groups would be four feet six inches, yet most youngsters at ten are either above or below that average.

To reject children as created is to find fault with their Creator. I can still feel the chills running up my spine when, as a school principal, I heard the mother of one of my students defiantly declare, "I might accept the fact that my daughter is average, but I will never accept the fact that she is *below* average."

To be certain of our evaluation, the girl's counselor and I examined her school records and reviewed all test scores related to her learning ability. We tried to explain to the mother that her daughter was working up to her (below-average) ability level. That's difficult to say to a concerned and disappointed parent.

It's natural for parents to want their offspring to excel, yet whenever mothers and dads pressure a child to be tops in selected endeavors, they can harbor unrealistic expectations and act unlovingly toward the child and toward others who are trying to help. That kind of parental attitude is about as rational as insisting that a Volkswagen perform with the power of a Cadillac. Children long to be accepted as they are, not because of their gifts or lack of them.

The late psychologist Paul Tournier claimed that in every child's heart lies an inexhaustible need to be loved. In all of their human relations and activities, Tournier believed, children yearn for proofs of acceptance and love from their parents more than from other people. When children doubt their worth, it is hard to convince them that those most significant in their lives really do love them.

IT'S LONELY AT THE BOTTOM

Most kids will never become top scholars, winners of beauty contests, or high-paid athletes. Some will never be serious competitors in any of these areas.

Take ten-year-old Andrew. His classmates considered him "different." Skinny and uncoordinated, he was always chosen last for any competitive sport. At gym class his teammates would moan, "Do we have to put Andrew on *our* team?" Claire, a high school sophomore, was short and fat with thick ankles, a face full of freckles, and poor self-esteem. She longed to be tall and slender with shapely legs like her classmates. She pored over ads that promised: "Lose unwanted fat!" but feelings of guilt increased each time she tried to diet and failed.

Children like Andrew and Claire who are shut out by their peers need acceptance, affection, and reassurance from family members and friends.

SCARS TO PROVE IT

Counselors struggle to salvage the damaged lives of children who are disabled by destructive parenting. Susan Forward, in her book *Toxic Parents*, reports:

> **A solid majority [of my clients] have suffered a**
> **damaged sense of self-worth because a parent had**
> **regularly hit them, or criticized them, or "joked"**
> **about how stupid or ugly or unwanted they were, or**
> **overwhelmed them with guilt, or sexually abused**
> **them, or forced too much responsibility on them, or**
> **desperately overprotected them.**[1]

Many of Dr. Forward's clients were astonished to realize the enormous impact their early child-parent relationships still had on their malfunctioning as adults.

"WHAT'S A PARENT TO DO?"

How can parents increase their children's healthy self-esteem? The twin secrets are: (1) regularly demonstrate love and respect, and (2) show your children how to defuse the negative elements in their lives that destroy high self-esteem. Work on these before your children reach their teens; the results of early parental abuse or neglect are even more difficult to eradicate after the age of twelve.

Even if a parent has been negligent in the past, it's never too late to begin corrective action. With God's help, genuine parental love can effect extraordinary changes.

"I DON'T HAVE TIME NOW"

Given the pace of modern life, today's parents on the average devote less time to their children than the generation that preceded them. One reason is that many adults spend much of their time at home sitting in front of a television set. We might not love our children any less, but we frequently choose watching TV instead of investing personal time with our kids. What does an I-don't-have-time-for-you attitude say to a child?

Many parents are workaholics. Do you recognize one in your mirror? An obsession for work inside or outside the home tends to devalue the worth of a child. It says to a youngster, "You're less important than the work I have to do."

Ignored children will find ingenious ways to gain recognition. They'll demand a parent's notice by testing every boundary a family establishes. When starved for parental attention, children will often choose irritating conduct, even though it triggers their parents' wrath. Overlooked children would rather be yelled at or punished than ignored by the people they regard as highly significant in their lives.

When moms and dads figure out how they will spend their time, children often get a very small portion. Parents who define success in terms of dollars earned plus prestige in the community often neglect to cultivate warm and happy relationships with their children. Teenagers in particular need caring parents who will listen and offer guidance. We can learn from Lee Atwater, the late Republican National Committee chairperson. When seriously ill prior to his death, Atwater declared, "I thrived on status and wealth, but now I'd trade everything I gained in exchange for more time with my children."

THE NEED FOR TIME TOGETHER

Ask young children what makes a happy home and many will answer, "It's doing things together as a family." Children hardly ever list material possessions such as money, cars, or a fine house. With both parents often away at work, spending adequate time with children requires careful planning.

When one of our daughters was in high school, I learned an important lesson: When children cry out for a parent's attention, Mom or Dad will either give it or live with regrets a few years later. This daughter always came home a little late from parties or dates. Only years later when my wife and I reviewed the situation did we realize what our daughter's needs were.

Since my work schedule was heavy and my time with this daughter inadequate, she found a way to get my full attention. When she came in late, I would be waiting up to discuss her infraction. Typically we'd talk for half an hour or more on a variety of topics. My wife, in bed by that hour, worried that we must be engaged in long disagreements.

Years later, our daughter commented to her mother, "When I went away to college, I really missed you and Dad—especially those long, wonderful talks Dad and I used to have late at night." Finally the light dawned! Our daughter had gained my attention and time by ignoring the family curfew, an act to which I responded without fail. In this way she could assure herself of her workaholic father's undivided attention. Today, I realize that I was truly blessed to have a teenager who did not sever our relationship, who still wished to talk with me. Parents need to take seriously a child's need to have uninterrupted time with each of them.

I was delighted recently to learn why a busy investment counselor had not been in his office when I tried to contact him. He had taken his son on a salmon fishing trip for the boy's tenth birthday. On the way home his son looked up to him, smiled contentedly and said, "Dad, that was the funnest time I ever had."

Positive parenting requires that we make time for some special events that a child may cherish for a lifetime. We certainly need to modify the statistic I heard recently that half of all fathers spend less than fifteen minutes a week with each of their adolescents.

Enhancing a child's self-worth is a parent's most challenging mission, and one that does not take excessive time. Doing this well affects not only the life of your child but also the lives of children in generations to come. Parental attitudes and actions in the home determine whether a child feels loved or unwanted, worthy of respect or a worthless disappointment. Each child's level of self-esteem is shaped largely by parents who take the time to love or ignore the child God created and placed in their care.

WHY KIDS RUN AWAY

When teenagers feel that no one at home cares about them, they may decide to leave. Many a youth on the street cites a lack of family communication at home as the major reason for running away. Other reasons for abandoning home and family include: (1) wanting to escape continual criticism, (2) fearing family fights due to drug and alcohol abuse, and (3) evading physical or sexual abuse.

We may think young people leave home because they dislike parental controls, but surveys seldom show that as the primary reason. One high school girl lamented to a counselor: "When I moved out of my home, I was convinced that my parents had too much control over me. After living on the streets for a while, I began to appreciate the rules and limits I had at home."

IMPARTIALITY

James Dobson for many years was assistant professor of pediatrics (child development) at the University of Southern California School of Medicine in Los Angeles before founding the radio outreach called "Focus on the Family." Dobson believes that the current epidemic of self-doubt has resulted from a totally unjust and unnecessary system of evaluating human worth. He writes:

> **Not everyone is seen as worthy; not everyone is accepted. Instead, we reserve our praise and admiration for a select few who have been blessed from birth with the characteristics we value most highly. It is a vicious system, and we, as parents, must counterbalance its impact. . . . All children are**

created worthy and must be given the right to personal respect and dignity.[2]

INSIGHTS FOR PARENTS

1. Being an effective parent is one of life's most demanding and rewarding tasks. Is any responsibility more important than helping to shape a human life during its tender and teachable years?

2. "An unloved child is the saddest phenomenon in all of nature."—James Dobson

3. Low self-esteem affects all aspects of life. Being fearful of rejection, youngsters find it difficult to communicate their feelings to their parents and friends.

4. Every child's birthright should include a guarantee of quality time with each parent. The amount and quality of the time we willingly invest reveals the level of our commitment to a child.

5. A child with low self-esteem struggles with a sense of incompleteness, with inner feelings that range from self-doubt to self-hatred.

6. Criminologists believe that delinquent behavior frequently develops in youth with a poor self-image who feel obligated to show off and "perform" for friends.

7. Young children whose parents are warm, loving, and accepting will probably turn out to be adolescents who possess self-respect.

8. Consistent love is a particularly indispensable requirement for infants, children, youth, the middle-aged, and the elderly; in other words, for everyone.

```
┌─────────────────────────────────┐
│          THINGS TO DO           │
└─────────────────────────────────┘
```

Try these activities with your children and then, if possible, share them in a parents' group or informally with friends who are parents.

A. Hold a family inventory session where you and your children identify and record favorite things you do together. Don't overlook simple but meaningful events such as family devotions. Ask your children which activities they enjoy the most. Schedule time for those activities you see as most bonding.

B. Review and update the list periodically. Attend carefully to each child's suggestions for new family-togetherness activities.

C. Schedule another family discussion session where each member is asked to think of, and share, two special qualities they like in each of the others. If desired, add time for asking a question, such as, "Can you tell us why you like the particular qualities you've chosen?" This session may develop into one of your most tender and loving family experiences.

3

When Children Are
Belittled and Discounted

Love is the basic need of human nature.

—Dr. Karl Menninger

The eighth amendment of the United States Constitution, written in 1791, prohibits excessive bail, excessive fines, and "cruel and unusual punishment." To hear some parents speak about their children, you'd think they have forgotten these provisos for behavior which "we the people" are supposed to follow.

I was astonished one day to hear a student tell me at a social event, "I'm the ugly one." Never had I heard anyone make such a demeaning statement about herself. Curiosity prompted me to ask Elicia about her early childhood.

"My father often says how homely I am," she said. "Then he complains, 'I'll never be able to save enough money to get you married off!' "

Those tapes of her father's cruel remarks continue to play in Elicia's mind, and the hurt is never far away.

Barry had similar childhood experiences. He commented in a youth discussion group, "I'm sure that most of us accept as true anything a parent says over and over again."

He paused for a few moments to regain his composure, then continued: "I feel I am worthless to my mother. All my life she kept telling me I was incompetent. I can still hear her shouting, 'Can't you ever do anything right? You're just plain worthless around here!' Those words still echo in my head. There is no way I can shake my feelings of worthlessness. How I wish she would say just once that she loves me."

As Barry discovered, feelings of low self-esteem, once embedded in the mind, defy change.

WHO NEEDS ENEMIES?

Moms and dads are not always diplomatic when discussing with outsiders the faults and weaknesses of their children. I'm sure they don't intend to be hurtful, but they can thoughtlessly bruise their child's self-image with inconsiderate remarks.

In a supermarket I once overheard two mothers discussing their children. As I listened, the mother with a small son standing nearby said to her friend, "Brandon here has always been slow in school. The doctor said that he may have been brain-damaged at birth. We're not sure about that, but he'll never be a good student like his sister."

Regardless of Brandon's other unique talents and abilities, that mother may discover that her son will probably never work up to his potential.

A building contractor remembers his father, whom he could never please. If he did well in high school football, his father needled him for not joining the school tennis team. If he went out for baseball, his father criticized him for not playing the position he wanted his son to play. Finally the boy ran away and refused to talk to his father.

Children's early feelings of self-esteem often plummet when they become teenagers. Such concerns intensify each time a young person compares himself or herself with peers or media models who are better looking, more intelligent, or more athletic. When we belittle our children, they feel even more like dummies or dreadful disasters—like "ugly" Elicia or "worthless" Barry.

SILENCE CAN HURT

Not until her grandfather's funeral did my friend Lora learn of her dad's secret hurt. After the burial service, her father lingered at the graveside. Finally he broke down and stammered in utter dejection, "Dad never once told me he loved me—never!"

I can understand that father's anguish. That most important expression, "I love you, Kenneth," was not a part of my childhood experience either. More regrettably, I always felt uncomfortable about trying to verbalize the affection I felt for my children. I've always loved each of them dearly, yet I wonder: Did my inability to clearly express my feelings of love make it more difficult for my children to perceive the love of our heavenly Father? Fortunately, each of them heard their mother tell of our love over and over. Today they, too, are able to express their love for all family members.

THE ABUSE OF NEGLECT

John Gardiner shared what he overheard three boys saying as he walked through his clinic one day. The first said that his mom always yelled at him. The second complained that his dad hit him. The third and more forlorn-looking of the three slowly commented that his dad didn't even hit him.

"Often the worst thing that can happen to a human being is to be isolated and ignored," wrote Gardiner.[1]

A few years ago I received permission from authorities to visit our county jail and talk with inmates about their early home experiences. One prisoner told me, "I was eighteen when I first got busted. It was late December, so I thought I'd call home with some Christmas wishes. My dad answers the phone and says, 'Where the heck are you?' I says, 'I'm in jail.' He hands the phone to my sister and refuses to even talk with me. That hurt. He could have bailed me out but after how he acted, I knew there was no way. Mom did visit me several times, but Dad has written me off. To him, I don't exist anymore."

Neglect is abuse. If our actions as adults send a message of rejection to youth, we're really saying, "Don't bother me with any of your problems. I have more important things to do. Face it. You are low on my list of priorities."

Intentional or not, such emotional bruising can inflict life-long resentment and pain. A child will eventually conclude, "I'm a zero in my own home, unwanted by my own parents."

All children yearn for continual assurances that they're acceptable and precious individuals—that their earthly parents, as well as their heavenly Father, love them in tender, special ways.

Consistent cherishing by parents heals emotional hurts and nurtures the child's positive sense of self-worth.

"ESAU HAVE I LOVED"

In Genesis, an intriguing part of the Abraham, Isaac, and Jacob stories is a father's preference for one of his twin sons. One of the twins, Jacob, succeeded in pretending to be Esau, the preferred twin, and obtained Isaac's blessing. Jacob went on to have twelve sons from whom the twelve tribes of Israel came into being.

So favoritism toward one child in the family is nothing new. A parent might deny favoritism, but it is hard to camouflage from siblings. A surprisingly large percentage of children are convinced that another child was their parents' darling.

Occasionally, that's true. Still, most moms and dads struggle not to give any evidence of such preferences if they do exist.

"Daddy calls Dolly 'Princess,'
so why doesn't he call
me 'Prince'?"

Martha was participating in a seminar whose theme focused on childhood experiences that boosted or bruised one's feelings of self-worth. Eventually, Martha shared a lifelong sorrow that still festered in her heart. After her youngest sister was born, she told us, nearly all of her father's attention was focused on Bessie. Bessie was a beautiful child with flawless complexion, curly hair, and a winning smile. All the siblings agreed that Bessie was their father's darling.

Years later the father became seriously ill. He was comatose at times and not expected to live. Although Bessie was unable to return, Martha traveled home for a last visit. Still yearning for her father's love, Martha took his hand.

Enfeebled and confused, the father grasped Martha's hand tightly and murmured, "My dearest Bessie. It's so wonderful of you to come and be with me now! You know how special you've always been to me."

At this point in her story Martha broke into uncontrollable sobbing. Other seminar members reached out to Martha. Some enfolded her in their arms. Finally Martha sighed, "It's such a deep pain. I've never been able to talk about it before. And I've never been able to forget it, either."

Most of us can truthfully state that we would never engage in such blatant partiality. Yet it's often more difficult to love a child who has inherited some personal traits that we dislike in ourselves. Likewise, it's natural for a parent to be extra fond of a youngster who happens to manifest the qualities the parent has always admired in a much-loved spouse. As a result, even conscientious parents who strive to treat each child equally may unwittingly fall into a trap of favoritism.

Linda Mouat believes that a similar bias can also develop in a family where one child has a chronic illness or disability. Parents, as well as friends, normally become so concerned and involved with the needs of the suffering child that they are less aware of the minimal attention they give to siblings who are well. A healthy child can often be found sitting on the sidelines while the sick child gets extra attention, expressions of concern, and gifts.

"We've learned the painful way," writes Ms. Mouat, "that the other children in the family also need attention and love from family, friends and church families."[2]

HUMILIATION REINFORCES SELF-DOUBTS

Stan can still feel his embarrassment at the age of seven when his mother humiliated him in front of family and friends.

"Because I was a bedwetter, my mother dressed me in a towel pinned on as a diaper. Then she made me take out the garbage in front of all our neighbors. I was positive my mom didn't love me," Stan says.

Shame diminishes any child, particularly one who especially needs some evidence of a parent's love and acceptance. Victims like Stan conclude, "I must be awful or my mother would never disgrace me like this." Once such a degrading experience roots itself in an individual's "inner child," it continues to operate like a videotape that automatically replays whenever that person feels down on himself.

"I JUST DON'T MEASURE UP"

Children often compare their personal weaknesses with a friend's perceived strengths. They not only underestimate their own qualities but typically overestimate another's attributes and disregard that person's problems and failures. Some adolescents have told me they have little to live for because they don't excel in some peer-approved qualities. When they are disappointed with themselves, their self-esteem crumbles.

Consider physical appearance. High school counselors report to parents that eight of ten teenagers in the United States are discontented with their looks. This attitude is often the result of an actual or perceived physical imperfection.

A large percentage of media advertising is aimed at children. By the time of high school graduation, a typical young person has been engulfed by five thousand hours of advertising. Unfortunately, its major purpose has been to indoctrinate youth with the philosophy that abundant material possessions, including the "right" clothes, will guarantee that they will be popular and happy. One result is the brand-name jungle in most schools. Convincing commercials have sold the kids on the belief that anyone who fails to wear clothes with trendy labels will suffer peer rejection.

PARENTS WHO DISCOUNT THEMSELVES

Advertising is not the only agent responsible for self-discontent among young people. They also learn it from their parents. Some parents feel called upon to bad-mouth their own abilities or lack of them with comments like, "I've always been clumsy," or "I'll blow it, I know I will!" or "I've never been good at (whatever)."

Studies suggest that many adults also depreciate their own appearance. Think about all those who would like to reshape their noses or get a tummy-tuck or have hair implanted on their balding domes or develop larger busts, bigger eyes, more oval faces, or smoother skin. Many men would choose broader chests, more prominent chins, and less protruding ears. Before you are tempted to reshape your God-given physique, stop and think: Does your self-disparaging lead to similar self-discounting practices in your children?

A good friend of mine is a member of a medical school faculty. On the subject of self-depreciation, he told me, "My major source of low self-esteem is self-criticism. First, I expect too much of myself. Then I beat myself over the head when I can't live up to my grand expectations. To make sure I'm liked, I strive to please others under any and all circumstances, regardless of my personal limitations. I tell myself that I should be able to help more of my patients, be of more assistance at home, spend more time with my children, and on it goes. The more I talk to myself this way, the lower my self-esteem sinks. Then if someone is critical of me in any way, that only aggravates my personal attitude problem. I never realized before that my kids might be learning how to discount themselves by watching me."

Many children struggle to meet grandiose expectations imposed by parents, by peers, and by themselves. Young people need to understand that only a small fraction of their friends are naturally witty, bright, well coordinated, or highly popular. The majority are ordinary, everyday kids with equally strong needs to be accepted and loved. In the final analysis, we should work to assure our children that a healthy way to live, a way that is good for our self-esteem, is to accept ourselves as God already accepts us—no more and no less.

THE PERMANENT "SOLUTION"

Some, unable to rise above their disappointments, are shattered by them.

A boy penciled the following note at home after school: "This is the last note I shall ever write. No one should feel bad about my going as I am not worth it. I don't want to go but there is nothing else to do. I've never been much good."[3]

A child who can't meet his or her parents' expectations may feel hopeless. Young people often conclude they have not only disappointed their parents but also sabotaged all hopes for a successful future.

A high school girl came into my office one day and told me in anguished tones, "Last year my older sister was inducted into the Honor Society, but I just failed to get in. I'll never be able to earn a college scholarship now. I'm afraid to go home and face my parents. They'll really blow up at me."

Another teenager in a similar situation also encountered unreasonable parental pressures to excel. He wrote the following note to his closest friend:

"My parents want me to be the best at everything but I've let them down. I can't possibly please them. I'll miss you. Goodbye."

Statistics on young people who consider self-destruction are shocking. Teenage suicide in some cities has doubled annually for the last few years. Among students nineteen years old and younger, suicide is now believed to be the third most common cause of death. Many of these young people conclude that self-inflicted death is preferable to feeling unwanted by their parents and unacceptable to their peers.

An inability to excel in ways that gratify a parent is a major factor that can contribute to a teenager's thoughts of self-destruction. Such home pressures may include playing on an athletic team, becoming a beauty queen, qualifying for the honor roll, or gaining admission to a prestigious university or social group.

What might ultimately cause a young person to ask, "Is life really worth living?" Sometimes it doesn't take much. An exhausted father arriving home from work may angrily berate his son. Unfortunately, the son does not stop to think, "Dad must have had a hard day at the office. He really doesn't mean those awful things he's yelling at me." Instead, the young man typically blames himself. He concludes, "Dad wouldn't say those awful things if there wasn't something wrong with me. He thinks I'm terrible!"

Mothers and fathers forget how fragile children are. Continual criticism or abuse, with little or no positive affirmation, can sow the seeds of a child's self-destruction. Those with desperately low self-esteem may conclude, "Death appears to be the only way out of my misery."

Authorities on teenage suicide in the United States claim that each year, more than five thousand teenagers kill themselves, and half a million more make an attempt to do so. For those between the ages of five and fourteen, suicide is the sixth leading cause of death. Between the ages of fifteen and twenty-four it's the leading cause. Worse yet, the rate of suicide for teenage mothers is seven times greater than that for other teenagers.[4] Their personal agony is dreadful enough, but each death also leaves behind distraught parents, bewildered siblings, and grieving friends.

A recent study found that family discord was one reason for attempted suicides cited by youth who survived. We need to remember, however, that some young people who consider suicide come from stable, relatively happy families. Their reasons are complex and often include mental and emotional stresses of unknown origin. What parents can do is to be alert to their children's depression or unhappiness, listen to their kids, show them how much they love them, and seek professional help for them if their depression continues.

Many high school counselors and administrators say that suicide-prone students often have no one at home who takes time to listen to them. Such parents don't realize the importance of setting aside regular time for in-depth communication with each child. When at-risk youth experience criticism, humiliation, or neglect, they feel let down by the very persons who brought them into the world.

```
INSIGHTS FOR PARENTS
```

1. Parents need to help their children realize that God knows them better than they know themselves, and that God loves them better, too.

2. "The worst sin toward those close to us is not to hate them, but to be indifferent to them."—George Bernard Shaw

3. Discounting ourselves or our children teaches them to discount themselves and others. This fosters persistent feelings of worthlessness.

4. Lack of love for a child often says more about a parent's inability to love than it does about the child's lovableness.

5. "A healthy self-image is seeing yourself as God sees you—no more and no less."—Josh McDowell

6. Humiliating a child may satisfy a parent's need to feel superior but can severely damage a child's self-esteem.

7. Suicide is the acting-out of an extreme sense of personal worthlessness and hopelessness. To counteract such tragedies, parents need to assure every child in their home and church family of their unfailing acceptance and love, not only from the parents but also from God, their heavenly Father.

8. Moms and dads who say "yes" to a child whenever possible will make the occasional "no" easier to accept.

9. If our parents used words as weapons against us, we need to be alert or we might perpetuate similar attacks and wound our children.

10. ". . . encourage one another and build one another up . . . help the weak and be patient with them all." —1 Thessalonians 5:11, 14 (RSV).

```
THINGS TO DO
```

Discuss the following issues with your spouse or with some other parents. First, identify several unrealized, often unintentional, ways moms and dads may discount a child's self-worth. Then use some or all of these questions to get your discussion started.

A. Did an unplanned child early in your marriage compli-
cate your life? Can you detect any lingering resentments toward
that child, feelings that might be difficult to control in times of
stress? Pray for a full release from any continuing prejudice that
may prevent you from completely accepting a blameless child
of God.

B. Can you individually, or as a group, think of examples
in which you have served as models of self-discounting that your
children may copy? Think carefully but candidly about such a
possibility.

C. While parents wish to be impartial and to avoid prefer-
ring one child over another, in what respects might one child in
your family feel less wanted than another? What about the child
most like you, or the child most like your spouse? An awareness
of such possibilities is the first step toward reconciliation.

D. Imagine you are able to eavesdrop on your children and
their friends when they are listing what their mothers and fathers
do that convinces them that they love them. What would your
children most likely say? What would you like them to say in
the future?

4

When Children Are
Loved and Cherished

To help a child see herself as good
is to encourage her,
almost in spite of herself,
to become so.

—Charlotte M. Yonge

As a boy, writer-pastor Walter Wangerin loved to throw rocks. He knocked over cans, connected with telephone poles, set birds to flight, and made bull's-eyes of whatever took his fancy.

High over the athletic field of the college where his father served as president, large six-thousand-watt bulbs circling the stadium made a tempting target for Walt's geological missiles. There wasn't one chance in a thousand that his rocks would smash one of those expensive lights, so he kept firing at them and watching his rocks glide harmlessly back to earth.

One day that thousandth rock connected. Glass exploded from the bulb and rained down on the field. No one else was around to see it, but Walt knew he had to confess his misdeed to his father. As he entered his dad's office, the big oak desk seemed to rise accusingly, but for Walt there was no turning back. He finally stammered out his crime and waited for his punishment. After a long period of waiting, Walt saw his father get up out of his chair, walk slowly around the desk toward him and then, as Walt explains it, "Dad killed me with a hug. I'll never forget that experience."

To the young man, it was an example of what it's like to have a loving Father in heaven, one who is willing to forgive his own children when they fail because the penalty has been paid.

My friend Lou was not as fortunate. In spite of his significant accomplishments and his unselfish service to others, Lou keeps putting himself down. His impoverished self-image spoils the enjoyment and sense of fulfillment he could have from the good things he is doing.

Recently Lou told me that throughout his painful childhood his father spent no time affirming Lou's work or acknowledging his kindnesses. "Dad was never satisfied with anything I did," he said. "What hurt most were the times when he'd look at me in disgust and mutter, 'You little rat!' My dad's words have festered inside me all my life. I always try to appear confident on the outside but inside lives a hurting little boy with a forlorn self-image. How can I ever forget that I was repulsive to my own father?"

Things were no better for Lou at church: "Our pastor would talk about a loving heavenly Father. I wanted to believe that but I couldn't accept such a parental image. It may sound foolish, but I got my best understanding of what God's love might be like during a Christmas season as a small boy. A department store Santa pulled me onto his lap, wrapped his arms around me, and held me in his loving hug for a little while. What a significant experience that was for me! I remember it vividly to this day."

DAMNING WITH FAINT PRAISE

Parents who rarely say anything complimentary to their children come up with the excuse, "If I don't criticize them, they will know I appreciate them." The absence of reproach, however, is not the same as giving recognition and praise. As parents we are responsible also for every idle silence, for each failure to offer positive, affirming words that every child so desperately needs to hear.

Consider the implications for parents in a National Labor Relations Institute "Job Condition Study" that included the importance of commendation. Supervisors of employees were asked to rank the ten most important factors related to on-the-job satisfaction. The managers believed that workers would rank "full appreciation for work done" as eighth in importance. The employees, however, ranked it number one.

Many parents have similar misconceptions about the importance of affirmations of their children. The adults might seldom bother to praise the youngsters, while the children think about parental affirmation constantly and strive earnestly to please. Only when children are affirmed, recognized, and encouraged are they free to develop their God-given talents.

As one high school counselor advised parents, "If you want your children to improve, be sure they can overhear the good things you say about them to others."

THE UNIVERSAL YEARNING FOR RECOGNITION

What do young people lack at home that drives them toward the artificial, transitory sense of pleasure from alcohol, drugs, and other highs? Many are physically well-nourished but suffer emotional malnutrition. The parents of these kids tend to ignore the good counsel in Proverbs 3:27, "Do not withhold good from those to whom it is due [our children], when it is in your power to do it." This verse is an essential guideline for every loving parent.

While serving as a high school principal, I had many discussions with parents about their children. On one occasion I was reviewing a student's behavior problems with his father. I asked how he reacted when his son got into trouble at home. He quickly shot back, "I bust him one whenever he does something wrong."

Next I inquired how he responded when his son did something right. With no hesitation the father responded, "Nothing. He's *supposed* to behave." This dad withheld the appreciation his son both deserved and desperately needed.

On another occasion, a student was telling me of his frustrating home experiences. Douglas explained, "I can mow the whole yard, edge the flower beds, and sweep the driveways and walks. Yet when my dad drives in, he never sees the overall yard. He complains about a single clump of grass I may have missed somewhere. How I'd love to hear him say, 'The yard looks great, Doug. Thanks for your hard work!'" Busy parents easily forget that gratitude without words is gratitude that is never heard.

Recognition and praise are powerful boosters of a child's self-concept. It is essential that parents notice, delight in, and express sincere appreciation for a youth's achievements. Similarly, moms and dads should commend a child for improvements under way even though the final goal has not yet been achieved.

A vice-principal in our school advised parents to "try to catch your youngster doing something right." Once adopted, this simple procedure improves many strained child-parent relationships.

The experience of a teacher in our high school illustrates the far-reaching effects of negative mind-sets. After school one day she phoned Mike's mother to tell her about the good work her son had done that day. Suddenly the mother cut in with, "You've got the wrong number," and hung up.

The teacher double-checked the boy's name and phone number. Sure she'd been talking to the right parent, she dialed again. This time Mike's mother broke down and cried. "No one from school has ever phoned before unless there's been a problem," she said in a shaky voice filled with emotion. "You have no idea how I appreciate this call today."

Such commendations build both the parents' and the child's self-esteem.

"THIS LITTLE LIGHT OF MINE"

A neighbor's favorite childhood memory is his mother's often-repeated remark, "Andy, you are very special to me!"

"As a child," Andy recalls, "I needed more than merely the knowledge that I belonged to a household. I needed the assurance that I was treasured by my parents, and thank God I got it."

Other friends who "got it" from affirming parents enjoyed good self-esteem that kept them from unsavory associations and caused them to make the right choices at critical turns.

"We both love you just the way you are" is an affirmation that one man remembers from his parents.

"You always have my love—no strings attached," said another mother.

Other parental remarks that boost a child's self-esteem include these:

- "I'd like to know what *you* think about this idea."
- "I really appreciated your help."
- "What you think is important to us."

All children make mistakes, but if they sense an undergirding of genuine parental love and patience, they will be convinced that their parents truly care for them. If a child is clumsy or awkward, it is shattering when a parent snatches away the responsibility with a comment like, "No, no! You're doing it all wrong. Here, let me do it!" Impatience and mistrust cripple, rather than boost, a child's self-esteem.

THE "WRITE" CHOICE

Following a church council seminar that I had led, the administrator of that congregation told me she had made up her mind to write one letter of appreciation a week to some member in her church.

About a year later I phoned to find out the results.

"It was wonderful," she told me. "I missed writing a few times, but every person I wrote to thanked me in some way. Many had tears in their eyes when acknowledging my note—especially the elderly members. Several young people were astonished but pleased to learn that their work had been recognized as being important to the church family."

She added this significant comment: "I, too, have been blessed by a more caring relationship with many of our members."

The experience made two major impressions on my friend. "First," she said, "both children and adults want to know if they've made a contribution to another person's life. Second, an affirmation has a more lasting impact upon a person when it is written down. Spoken praise is appreciated, but it's usually more casual. A written note represents greater effort on the part of the giver and provides something tangible which the recipient can enjoy rereading again and again months and even years later."

Jim Girvan, a former college baseball coach, tells a fascinating story about how he encouraged a group of college students to share their personal commendations with teammates. Early one spring Jim was convinced that his team that year had great potential, even though they had lost their first three games. Members of the team were becoming increasingly edgy and began to blame each other for their losses.

Coach Girvan called a special team meeting to deal with the rising frustration among his players. He began by handing every player a set of three-by-five-inch note cards. Each card in the pack carried the name of a different teammate. Then he asked the team members to write a positive comment on separate cards about each player. Teammates were asked to personally distribute the cards before the next practice.

Jim's eyes lit up as he shared what followed. "Wow! What a difference! The men talked about the 'high' involved in getting twenty notes from fellow athletes commenting on their positive attributes and skills. The team attitude was transformed. Some players kept the cards in their lockers and reread them during the season. The experience demonstrated the power of dwelling on others' strengths rather than on their weaknesses."

That exercise was the turning point in the baseball team's season. Coach Girvan reported that his players went on to win their league's national championship that year.

ONCE MORE WITH FEELING

A humorist always gets a laugh when he tells his audience, "Try praising members of your family, even if it frightens them at first." Distributing care notes within a family circle is a wonderful way to foster goodwill and love among the people who mean the most to us. Write your positive feelings on cards or Post-It Notes. Place them on a mirror, in a lunch box, in a book someone is reading, on a car's dashboard, or wherever a family member will find them unexpectedly.

Examples of winning notes include:

- "Amy, our yard looks great with the leaves all raked up."
- "Every day we thank God for you, Jason."
- "Mom, that was the best Thanksgiving dinner ever!"
- "Our children are blessed to have such a caring, loving father. Thanks for the time you share with them, Bill. Love, Darlene."

The Apostle Paul approved such affirmation when he said, "Encourage one another and build up each other" (1 Thessalonians 5:11).

A close friend showed me a copy of a special letter he wrote when his son became a teenager. It's an excellent example for all parents who may wish to consider sharing similar feelings with children in their family. He wrote:

> **Can a father tell his son too often that he loves him? Ours is a special relationship, for there is only one person in this world that I can call "my son."**
>
> **I remember holding you on my lap and letting you grasp my fingers with your tiny hands as I pulled you up to a sitting position. And when you were a young child and I came home from the office exhausted, you'd come running into my arms. How I loved that! How I loved you then, and how very much I love you now.**

SAYING IT EYE TO EYE

A member of our church looks back on tough years growing up. "As a sensitive, lonely, and timid kid," he told me, "I found my early days very troubling. But a tough junior high gym teacher helped me like no one else.

"One day he called me out of gym class. At first I froze with fear, but to my surprise Coach looked me right in the eye and said, 'I know what you're going through at home, but I also know the kind of stuff you're made of. I not only have loads of respect for you but I also have great confidence in you. You're going to make it.' A timely, face-to-face encounter filled with that kind of reassurance can keep a disheartened young soul afloat."

The incident reminded my friend of Jesus' encounter with the rich young ruler. He added, "Jesus looked him straight in the eye with compassionate love. In fact, God does this for his children every day. He knows the trials we're facing, and the timing of his affirming love is perfect."

TAKE TIME TO ACCEPT A COMPLIMENT

How do your children see you react when someone affirms *you*? Do you model gracious acceptance of positive comments? Or do you rebuff the caregiver's praise with simulated modesty?

When offered an expression of sincere appreciation, our own rickety self-esteem may prompt us to disagree. It's easy to respond clumsily, "Oh, it was nothing. Anyone could have done it." Negative comments contradict the benefactor and deny a blessing the individual is seeking to bestow. Parents should demonstrate to their children that authentic love knows not only how to give but also how to receive. Billy Graham once said, "God has given us two hands—one for giving and the other for receiving." It's a divine paradox that the gracious acceptance of kindness is actually a gift of love. Caring parents will know not only how to express gratitude but also how to receive it graciously so that the giver is blessed as well.

The routines of daily life make it easy to take for granted those who are near and dear to us. If we could somehow have a day's notice before our death, we'd be jamming the phone lines seeking to share previously unexpressed love. It's impossible to carry out an act of kindness or to express our love too soon. We never know when it might be too late.

INSIGHTS FOR PARENTS

1. Don't neglect outward declarations of love on the assumption that children should be able to detect your undeclared love.

2. Children always put forth greater effort when encouraged than when criticized.

3. Children typically value themselves if they feel valued by their parents.

4. When affirming children, comment specifically on what they've done well and how good it makes you feel.

5. Gracious acceptance of another's compliment is actually a gift to the giver.

6. If someone paid you fifty cents for every kind word that is said in your family and collected twenty-five cents from you for every sharp word, would you be richer or poorer?

7. Appreciation and praise, like gold and diamonds, often owe their value largely to their scarcity.

Say It Now

If you have a tender message,
Or a loving word to say,
Don't wait till you forget it,
But whisper it today.

For these some hearts are breaking,
For these some loved ones wait,
So give them what they're needing
Before it is too late.

—Anonymous

THINGS TO DO

A. How many times can you recall specifically affirming or praising each member of your family this past week?

B. How many times this week can you recall criticizing or putting down some member in your family?

C. If the next twenty-four hours gave you your last opportunity to express the appreciation and love you feel for each family member, what would you say to each one?

D. All next week, resolve to be alert to specific things each child does right. Promptly express your appreciation, sharing how good the actions make you feel.

5

Practicing Good Communication

It is impossible to overemphasize the immense need we all have to be really listened to, to be taken seriously, to be understood.

—Paul Tournier

Each year, adults in the United States pay therapists more than a billion dollars to listen to them. At the same time, countless children long for someone to hear what they have to say. Failing to get such attention, many girls and boys begin to wonder whether their parents love them. Each day that passes without our taking time to listen to a child is a day we can never recapture.

Today's culture encourages us to ignore much that we hear. Flooded by sounds from TV sets, radios, and Muzak raining down from the ceilings of stores and restaurants, we've become specialists in tuning out. How many times have parents said to a child, "If I've told you once, I've told you a thousand times! Don't you ever listen?" Yet what kind of an example do we set for our children? The psalmist's lament applies to us: "They have ears, but do not hear" (Psalm 115:6).

THE IMPORTANCE OF LISTENING

A survey of 550 family therapists showed listening as the number one skill most needed in families. One big reason young people give for running away from home is a lack of family communication. A survey of three thousand high school students supports this conclusion. The top two messages young people want to share with their parents are: "Communicate with us more" and "Listen to us more."[1]

When I was a high school principal, a student named Stephanie wrote an English paper on the topic of communication. One paragraph stated, "I know that people communicate, but is parental lecturing and threatening really communication? I wish my parents would stop their one-way tirades and actually take the time to learn what I'm thinking."

On another occasion a shy student was standing outside my office door one noon hour when I returned from lunch. Recognizing Julie as a recent transfer from a detention facility, I invited her to come in so we could get acquainted.

She entered slowly and sat down by my desk. I asked how I might be of help. "I've written a letter to my parents," Julie began, "and I wonder if you think I should give it to them or not."

I accepted her letter and read the following message:

> **Dear Mom and Dad,**
> **I'm sorry I've been such a headache for you this past year. I guess you have a right to wonder why I've seemed like an ungrateful trouble-maker after all the presents and nice clothes you always buy for me. But ever since I was a little kid, I've wanted to talk with you about many things, but you always seem too busy to listen. Many times I just go to my room, hide in my closet, and cry.**
> **When I got older, I finally realized that when I got into some trouble then you'd pay attention to me. You'd even take time to listen to me. Now I realize that was the wrong thing for me to do and I want to tell you I'm sorry.**
> **Love from your daughter,**
> **Julie**

Julie sat staring at the floor. When I finished reading, she looked up and asked, "Do you think I should give that to my mom and dad?"

After we talked more about Julie's home background, I said her parents should be pleased to receive such a sincere letter of explanation and apology. We also reviewed other ways she might share her need to talk with, and be heard by, her mom and dad.

She went home that evening determined to deliver her letter. I prayed that her parents would respond by making some changes.

When parents neglect their children's communication needs, the parents function as little more than robots, mechanically furnishing food, clothing, and shelter. Forlorn youth, deprived of needed companionship, soon become resentful and convinced they're unloved. They retaliate in devious ways, often by sabotaging whatever the parents try to do.

At times as parents we need to speak up and voice our convictions. At other times we need to shut up and listen to and understand what our young people are trying to share. We can offer our children no greater gift than our example of undivided attention and genuine interest in what they are saying.

HARMFUL LISTENING HABITS

Parents' failure to attend to what a child is trying to tell them damages the child's self-esteem. It's equally frustrating to a child when Mom or Dad listens briefly to what the child is saying and then cuts in with, "What you should do is. . . ." Children long for adults who carefully attend to their words and feelings with respect.

One of the most aggravating things parents do is jump to a guilty verdict before hearing a child out. Such injustice stings. Our actions imply, "Why should I listen? I can't believe you anyway." This is a blow to a child's self-esteem. When a parent is emotionally agitated, it's appropriate to explain, "I'm too upset to deal with this right now. Let's talk about it after dinner."

Attentive listening is required for any two-way communication. A friend admitted he had a habit of browsing through the newspaper whenever he "listened" to his son. His longtime practice of avoiding eye contact had convinced Ryan he had nothing worthwhile to share. Eventually my friend changed his behavior. Now he lays the paper aside and looks directly at his son when Ryan talks to him. In effect, he's listening with his whole being. He also refuses to interrupt Ryan even when inclined to do so.

"I've quit faking attention," Ryan's dad says. "Instead, I have an attitude that communicates, 'Tell me more. I care about you and I want to understand what it's like to be in your shoes.'"

"You hafta listen to me with your eyes,
Daddy. Not just your ears."

LISTENING WITH COMPASSION

A child needs active, not passive, listening at home. Like adults, children are filled with strong emotions they often suppress. Joan Borysenko writes,

> **We need the help of supportive others who can listen to us with compassion and allow us to express what we feel. Good listeners hear empathetically without belittling, without dictating what we should or shouldn't feel, without cutting us short by dispensing advice, and without trying to comfort us instead of hearing us out.[2]**

Careless communication in a family can be costly. Most school personnel have encountered parents who verbally abuse and seldom listen to their children. Borysenko claims that many young people considering suicide reached that desperate situation because no adults were available to listen to what they needed to share.

"I" MESSAGES VERSUS "YOU" MESSAGES

Family communication is more rewarding when parents use "I" statements instead of "you" accusations when they talk with their children. It's always tempting to send "you" messages and put the blame on another person when something goes wrong: "*You* made me drop the salad bowl. . . ." "It's *your* fault I got this traffic ticket. . . ." "This happened because *you* had to be a hero. . . ." And often the "you" accused is a child.

Responding instead with "I" messages eliminates the accusatory tone and fosters goodwill. Notice how much less blame is implied when these statements are substantiated for the accusations above:

- "*I* get nervous and jumpy whenever someone sneaks up behind me and yells."
- "When *I'*m driving in traffic, *I* get very distracted when there's so much commotion in the back seat. Now we'll have to figure out where the money for my traffic ticket will come from."
- "*I* thought it was a good idea when you first suggested it, but who could have known. . . ."

Pointing out the effect of a child's behavior is less damaging than suggesting that the child is to blame for the parent's actions.

Parents who use "you" statements will generally find their messages less effective because they generate negative, rather than cooperative, reactions. If a parent assigns blame, the child immediately tries to shift it elsewhere and the battle is on. By contrast, "I" messages prompt a more honest response from the child about his or her feelings. They also help children learn to consider another person's emotions and needs.

TEACHERS IDENTIFY COMMUNICATION BARRIERS

Classroom teachers spend more of their working time communicating than do most other adults. As a school administrator,

I requested teachers to identify unhelpful communication practices that adults should avoid. Their list of the most detrimental communication traits follows:

- Interrupting during a conversation.
- Minimal listening—letting your mind wander.
- Being judgmental—unwilling to see another person's point of view.
- Making up your mind before you hear all the facts.
- Belittling the other person's remarks.
- Criticizing individuals publicly.
- Failing to express any appreciation or to give credit.

COMMUNICATION TIPS FOR PARENTS

One of the best ways for parents to share their love is to listen to their children. Doing so demonstrates respect and caring. An attentive attitude says, "Because you are important to me, what you think and feel are also important."

"I didn't even ask my question!"

To enhance your parent-child relationships, select several of the following guidelines that you believe will give the most help to your family:

- When listening, periodically express in your own words what you perceive to be the central meaning of your child's comments. You may choose to say, "I want to understand what you are saying. Is this what you're thinking?" and then offer your paraphrase of the child's message. Simple feedback requires that you say very little, but such questions will foster more accurate understanding.

- Frequently use brief, noncommittal responses that encourage your child to say more. Examples include "I see," "I'd like to hear more about it," "Then what happened?" and "That was really important, wasn't it?"

- Be alert to what your child says nonverbally. Watch for physical cues that may be more significant than the words shared.

- Look a child in the eye while listening. To avoid eye contact is to appear uninterested in what the child says. She soon gets the feeling that her words aren't worth your attention.

- Compliment a child for every evidence of good thinking. Tell how much you appreciate opportunities for the two of you to share thoughts.

- Always take time to communicate with a child who comes to you with questions. The child will never be more ready to listen.

- Resist the temptation to interrupt a child's sharing with moralizing "you" messages. This sabotages genuine communication. Trust your children to work through many of their own problems as you listen to them.

- When a child is small, get down on the same eye level for one-on-one communication. Consider how insignificant you would feel attempting to talk with someone ten feet tall.

- Make daily opportunities to listen to each child. Some parents schedule a longer weekly "talk-time" on the calendar. Then a child can look forward to a special time just with you.

- These remarks encourage a child to share thoughts:
  "How are things with you today?"
  "That's interesting."
  "Would you like to talk about it?"
  "How do you feel about what happened?"
  "I'd like to know what you think about it."
- On a birthday or other celebration, give a coupon good for a gift of time together. Make it a notable experience shared by just the two of you.
- Finally, realize what an inadequate substitute a television set is for a parent. While the TV set talks, it never listens to your child. Neither can it hold your child's hand, give a hug, or say, "I love you."

INSIGHTS FOR PARENTS

1. Nothing is easier than talking, nothing as difficult as genuine communication.

2. "The first duty of love is to listen."—Paul Tillich

3. When we really listen to a child, empathy will help us to sense needs, anxieties, joys, and sorrows as if they were our own.

4. "The greatest problem in communication is the illusion that it has been achieved."—George Bernard Shaw

5. "Don't worry that your children won't listen to you; worry that they are always watching you."—Robert Fulghum

6. Parents need to be careful not to overdose a child's daily allotment of "vitamin Be Quiet."

7. There are times when parents need to speak up to be heard, but more often we need to shut up so we can listen.

8. "Everyone must be quick to listen, but slow to speak. . . ." (James 1:19, TEV)

THINGS TO DO

A. Meet and confer with several other parents. First ask each one present to identify and share the major problem experienced in communicating effectively with their children. Next, ask each to explain their best in-family communication techniques that they feel boost positive child-parent dialogue. Encourage questions to clarify any misunderstandings. Develop several suggestions for parent experimentation in the coming weeks.

B. Reconvene in several weeks. First share accounts of in-family communication improvements. Next, listen to those who experience continuing problems with their children. As a group, discuss the probable causes as well as possible corrective actions that could prove helpful.

6

What Our Actions Tell Our Children

**What we do speaks so loudly that children
don't hear what we say.**

Four backpackers had been hiking all day on a dusty wilderness trail in Washington's Cascade Mountains. At last they reached Holden Village, a former mining community and now a Christian retreat center near Lake Chelan. Youth workers in that village greeted the weary travelers in an unusual way. Instead of simply saying, "Hi, it's good to see you!" they invited the hikers to sit on a low rock partition. Then they brought out basins of water, soap, and towels. Kneeling down, they washed, dried, and massaged the hikers' tired feet. A spoken welcome could not have communicated the same love and concern for the weary travelers.

Many times words are not needed to express human emotions. How do you tell a baby you love it? Verbalizing alone has little meaning, yet cuddling, rocking, and comforting sounds are essential to the healthy development of an infant.

What parents communicate by actions usually reflects their attitudes more accurately than what is spoken. Studies reveal that whenever emotions are involved, more than half of the message comes through facial expression.

SILENT MESSAGES

Proverbs 6:13 talks about winking with the eyes, speaking with the feet, and teaching with the fingers, and it is true that our communication goes far beyond the words we say with our voices.

The eyes. St. Jerome said, "Without speaking, the eyes confess the secrets of the heart." We've seen children's eyes beam with delight beside the Christmas tree, fill with tears when leaving loved ones, open wide in surprise, or overflow with love. Ralph Waldo Emerson believed that people convey as much emotion with their eyes as with their tongues. Expressions of the eyes are a universal language.

Some parents have perfected a wounded glance to help control their child's behavior. Others resort to an icy, forbidding glare that warns, "Straighten up right now or you'll get it once we're home!"

When the cock crowed following Peter's third denial, Peter went out and wept bitterly, yet Jesus hadn't said one word to him. He simply looked straight at Peter with sorrowful eyes (Luke 22:60-62).

Eyes are a vital element in body language. When approaching another person, we normally look at each other until we're about eight feet apart, then we usually "dim" our eyes by turning them down or aside. In contrast, salespersons and beggars enhance their influence by seizing our gaze with theirs.

The mouth. The expression of the mouth often tells us more than the words it says. A ready smile radiates joy, warmth, and love; a forced smile communicates unwilling compliance; a sneer conveys contempt and scorn. Thrusting out the lower lip evidences pouting displeasure or a downcast feeling. A mouth with no expression or downward corners may indicate sadness. Lips tightly pressed together suggest tension, stress, or annoyance. These facial signs are understood by children as well as by adults.

Posture. Parents' posture in relating to their children is significant. If Mom or Dad slumps over or turns partially away, the child can tell that the parents are not very interested. Some adults peer down on children, talking at them from an "on-high" position of superiority. Other parents get down on the child's level and talk face-to-face. When children become adolescents, some parents still strive for a postural superiority by ordering them to "Sit down and listen to me!"

The feet. An interesting mental experiment is to assume that wherever you walk around your home, your feet leave visible trails that become more conspicuous the more frequently they're used.

As you mentally hover above your home and examine your tracks, what would you learn about your parenting practices? Do you *send* your children to bed, or do you *take* them to bed so you'll have an opportunity for some loving bedtime words and a prayer? Is the area outside your house or apartment building devoid of parental tracks, or is there evidence of your playing outdoor games with your children? Careful analysis of your travel patterns in and around the home will speak volumes, revealing whom you spend time with and whom you ignore.

The fingers. The verse from Proverbs mentions teaching with the fingers. How many times has your child seen a scolding index finger shaken in his face at home and at school? Are such adult habits helpful or demeaning to a child's self-concept?

READING UNSPOKEN CUES AND CLUES

A frail Bangladeshi woman came up beside me when I was walking in the market area of Dacca. The baby cradled in her left arm appeared frail and malnourished. Once the mother caught my attention, she locked her pleading gaze on my face. As we walked together she joined the fingertips of her right hand and moved them back and forth toward her mouth. Successful in making me aware of hunger, she next pointed several times to her baby's mouth. Neither of us knew the other's language, but her gestures had said it all.

Physical punishment is another example of an unspoken cue; it has a lasting and powerful influence on any child's self-esteem. Hitler's sister claimed that when Adolf was a boy, his actions provoked his father to such extreme harshness that he beat Adolf every day. Such wordless parental communication is both psychologically and physically devastating.

WORDLESS NEGLECT

Pleased with himself, one father informed me, "My children can never say that I laughed at them, denied them the latest clothing, or abused them. We have a sensible arrangement. We don't meddle in each other's affairs. They go their way and I go mine."

How will children interpret such a relationship? They will feel neglected and worthless. Parents who are preoccupied with possessions, job, and other personal interests leave in their wake children who yearn to be listened to, played with, and cherished. The silent message we give such children is loud and clear: You're not high enough on my priorities to warrant my time. None of us should be surprised at the activities of forsaken children who feel forced to seek attention elsewhere to make up for what they lack at home.

The average American watches four hours of television a day. Many home TV sets are turned on seven hours or more a day. Mothers and dads have succumbed to the temptation of "video-parenting," a practice that sabotages vital parent-child communication. A child's indiscriminate access to the teachings of TV can easily supersede parental teachings.

WORDLESS LOVE

"Your child needs your presence more than your presents," Jesse Jackson once said. Without a parent's presence, his or her presents won't mean much to the child.

How do we convince our children of our love, of God's love? Words help, but actions are stronger. Take stock of your allotted 1,440 daily minutes. How many do you share with your children? Even on busy evenings, do you take time to tuck your children into bed and to listen to what they have not had a chance to tell you that day? How often have they seen you frowning or agitated with them? How frequently have they seen your pleasant, encouraging smile?

Our loving touch also convinces children of our love and God's love. Frequent hugs and kisses, holding a little child on our lap, and other warm touches communicate much more than words alone. Chapter 12 takes a closer look at touch.

LEADING, NOT PRESCRIBING

Children watch every move their parents make—especially during their early, impressionable years. Parents want each child to acquire positive traits of honesty, responsibility, kindness, and respect for others. It is not easy, but the best way to teach these qualities is to model them.

When we are courteous to the checkout person in the supermarket, we show our children that other people count, even when we don't know them. If we have to help a child clean up spilled paints and do it without anger or negative remarks, the child may learn how to deal with later messes. Everyday tasks like doing the laundry, changing the cat litter, answering the telephone, and getting everyone ready to leave the house for church may say more to our children than we are aware.

Worship services, Sunday school, and family devotions can be helpful in giving children a good foundation, but words will never be as influential as the lives they watch us live each day.

In terms of outreach to others, how often do your children see you visit the homebound or the hospitalized? Have you encouraged your children and their friends to visit nursing home residents, perhaps to sing for them? Do you ever set a place at the table for an unexpected guest? Has your congregation adopted a needy family and enlisted children not only in helping choose food but also in sharing clothes and toys with them? How often have your children seen you helping with community service projects on homelessness, hunger, or illiteracy?

It's easy to overlook the lasting influence on children of both the positive and negative actions of parents. Parents may be unaware of their wordless messages, but impressionable youngsters constantly watch what adults do. As night follows day, children embrace and pass along what they have seen in the lives of grownups—whether a blessing or a curse. This adopting of our traits will be our most constructive, or our most heartrending, legacy to each child, to their children, and to the coming generations.

INSIGHTS FOR PARENTS

1. "A thousand words do not leave so deep an impression as a single deed." —Henrik Ibsen

2. Your work will wait while you show a child a rainbow, but the rainbow won't wait while you finish your work.

3. We cannot *not* communicate. When silent, even our inactions, as well as our actions, shout volumes.

4. The mediocre parent commands, the good one explains, and the great one shows and inspires.

5. Attend to your child's feelings as well as words. Watch carefully for body language that reveals emotions such as fear or confusion.

6. One positive example is worth more to a child than twenty barrels of advice.

7. Adolescents typically don't pay too much attention to what we say about our religion, but they watch what we do about it.

8. The following approach is helpful in working with a disobedient child: "I love you too much to let you behave in ways that hurt other people."

9. It is extremely difficult to train a child to behave in ways the parents do not behave. Too often the footsteps that a child follows are those that parents thought they had covered up.

10. The prayers expressed by the lives we live may be as effective as those we say on our knees.

THINGS TO DO

A. Estimate the amount of one-on-one time you spend with each child per day. Write that estimate and the child's name on a three-by-five-inch card.

For several days, record on the back of the card the number of minutes you actually spend with the child. Compare the results with your original estimate. With your spouse or another parent, reflect on and discuss the significance of the results. Are you satisfied with what you learned? Write your goal for the future on the front of the card and review your progress each week.

B. Try to set aside a time-out-for-listening period when you can give each child your undivided attention, even if the time isn't long. Let your child introduce any topics important to him or her.

C. Cherishing parents seek to have fun with their children. How much of your time with a child each week now qualifies as recreation and fun? Recognize the inevitability of a day not too distant when your child(ren) will no longer be with you. Have as few regrets as possible by making space for some family fun time now.

7

When There Are Wounds

It's easy to become a parent,
difficult to be one.

—Wilhelm Busch

grew up in a traditional two-parent family but without a close relationship with my dad. I never sensed that he loved me. When I felt rejected I never asked myself, "Is something troubling dad?" Instead I wondered, "What's wrong with me?"

"Anytime you're ready, Daddy, I'll be
sitting outside growing older."

How I yearned to have Dad play ball with me, roughhouse with me, take me for a walk, hold me in his lap, tell me he loved me. I can't say that my father never loved me. I can say that a combination of emotional abuse, physical punishment, and rejection left me with a disability—a battered sense of self-worth.

"SO THE NEIGHBORS WON'T HEAR"

Few adults want to disclose an unhappy home situation, yet to illustrate the lifelong impact of a parent's attitudes and actions, I must share a few early incidents from my childhood.

One of my most vivid images of boyhood focuses on the center hall of our house with all the doors shut so no sound would drift out of the windows and doors to pique the interest of neighbors. There my dad would paddle me while my mother held her hand over my mouth. Occasionally I would catch a glimpse of Mother shaking her head, her facial expression imploring Dad to stop. He was not inclined to stop, however, until he had spent his anger.

Such punishment was not the result of some malicious offense or disobedience, but rather of my violation of family standards for proper behavior at church. Parental pride required that my sister and I always reflect credit, never embarrassment, on our parents. Years later I realized that in his childhood home, Dad had learned that it was a father's duty to break a child's perverse nature and bring it under control.

In most parent-child conflicts, only the parent possesses the physical strength to have his or her way. But does might make right in a showdown? We parents may like to believe it does. In the process, however, a child's self-esteem can be greatly undermined.

Parents can crush a child's sense of self-worth by failing to distinguish between the misdeed and the child. It's damaging to say, "Look at what you've done! How could you be so stupid? You'll pay for this now!" Emphasis on wrathful punishment implants fear in the child's heart. How tragic to miss an opportunity to model God's forgiveness, which will bring not only loving pardon but peace and joy to a child.

Children can innocently trigger a parent's wrath. If Mom or Dad is already upset with the boss, the car, a neighbor, or the shabby work of some trusted employee, a child's untimely transgression may prove to be the latch that opens the floodgates of pent-up frustration. In such a situation, it's easy for the adult to become hostile, even abusive.

If you must punish your child, make certain that you make a distinction between the behavior that you reject and the child you still love. Kneel or sit beside your child. Lead her in a prayer that seeks God's forgiveness. Add your parental pardon. Seal the closure of the event with a healing hug. Then emphasize to your child that she is still a cherished member of the family.

THAT STOWAWAY CHILD WITHIN

Sarcastic words drive a wedge between a youth and the parent on whom he relies for love. The child who is not sure of a parent's love will move into adulthood with an inner stowaway child continually starving for attention and affection to fill that vacuum.

The National Family Institute reports that the average parent spends 14.5 minutes a day communicating with each child. Of that total, 12.5 minutes are spent in correction and criticism.

In her book *Guilt Is the Teacher, Love Is the Lesson*, Joan Borysenko writes:

> **Inside me there is a seven-year-old who is still**
> **hurting from her humiliation at summer camp. Her**
> **anguish is reawakened every time I find myself in the**
> **presence of an authority figure who acts in a**
> **controlling manner. At those moments my intellect is**
> **prone to desert me, and I am liable to break down**
> **and cry with the same desolation and helplessness I**
> **felt when I was seven.[1]**

The stowaway child that many adults carry continues to respond to others as it formerly did to parental words and actions. At a personal growth seminar I met one of these stowaways, two individuals in one: the observable individual was a university dean; the other was a child within. When they both surfaced in the meeting, I was better able to understand my own stowaway child.

On the first day of the seminar, Gordon and I were members of the same small discussion group. I soon began to resent this man for trivial reasons. Immediately Gordon assumed the role of leader in our group. He appeared to have unlimited self-confidence, something I lacked.

On the following day, Gordon joined another small group. In one of the activities, the other members of his group rejected his major recommendation. The seminar leader asked Gordon the discerning question, "How do you feel about your group's rejection?"

"No problem!" Gordon replied, smiling broadly.

"I find that a curious reaction," the leader persisted. "Normally when associates reject our thinking we feel put down."

Gordon stared at the floor and said nothing for a while. Then his persuasive, self-assured facade began to crumble. Finally he broke down and cried. Dabbing at his tears with his handkerchief, Gordon admitted, "Yes, my group's disapproval did hurt. All my life I've kept the feelings of inadequacy experienced by that small boy hidden inside me—a bruised stowaway from childhood days. I try to keep him concealed from others with a front of self-confidence."

Gordon's candor surprised me. I was deeply moved. I thought, "This guy is a normal human being after all! He's not that super, self-assured person I saw yesterday."

Then it was my turn to fight back the tears. Mine were tears of empathy for this genuine, hurting individual. Drawn by his honesty, I went over and put my arm around Gordon's shoulder. The bruised little boy who had just surfaced was no stranger to me. I'd been struggling for many years to conceal a twin brother of this stowaway. Now I not only understood Gordon but I admired him and hoped we'd be friends.

Adult feelings of inadequacy are well-kept secrets. When parents conceal their weaknesses, children who feel inadequate conclude, "I must really be terrible because my parents don't have problems like mine."

REPORT CARDS CAN LIE

Report cards tell it like it is—or do they? Does a low grade always mean that a student is not intelligent? If a teacher divulges behavioral problems, does that mean that the child is a rebel?

Before you decide, read the stories of two typical students in average schools of America:

Melissa had good parents, but her father could not tolerate any grade on her report cards but an A. If Melissa brought home anything less, she was harshly punished.

"I wasn't lazy or bad," she says, "but certain classes were harder than others and so my grades were lower than Dad liked."

If Melissa got anything lower than an A in conduct, her father would strike her with a board. Once in the sixth grade she took home two C's on her report card. This so enraged her father that he hit her seventeen times with the board. "A lot of me just turned into one big bruise," Melissa says.

In contrast to Melissa's severe punishment, my wife Lois had a different experience when she showed her mother a C grade on her report card. They sat down at the table and looked at it together.

"Well," said Lois's mother calmly, "a C is an average grade and that's OK if you did your best. Probably you can bring it up to a B next time—maybe even to an A later in the year."

And that's exactly what happened. It's not difficult to guess which of the two, Melissa or Lois, might still be harboring feelings of inadequacy as a result of a parent's overreaction.

ADULTS ABUSED AS CHILDREN

Six and one-half million children a year suffer physical abuse in the United States. That's an average of four mistreated children per classroom. It's also unsettling to hear a corrections official relate that 80 percent of felons say they were physically battered as children.

Because I was curious to find out for myself the level of self-esteem experienced by prisoners, I arranged to meet with a group of men and women inmates in our state penitentiary. After discussing general topics for a while, one perceptive woman volunteered, "I was definitely abused as a child. I think that's why I've accepted so much abuse as an adult. Apparently some part of me believes I deserve the cruelty. It's kind of like I have ill treatment coming because I'm not much good. At times I even wonder if I don't unconsciously seek abuse. I've often suffered swollen lips and blackened eyes. In spite of that fact, I always seem to go back to the same man. Now I'm working at liking myself more so when I get out of prison I won't need his brand of attention."

The woman seemed lost in thought for a minute. Then she continued, "I think that may be why God put me here—to help me build up my self-esteem so I won't have to let some guy abuse me in the future in order to get the attention I need."

Our group fell silent. After a while I said, "I'll pray for you and ask that God's love will make you strong enough not to need that kind of attention." After a pause, two other inmates turned her way. Each of them said, "I'll pray for you, too."

WHEN DIVORCE DIVIDES A FAMILY

When divorce divides a family, the children witness not only parental conflict but also the terrible threat that they might be abandoned. Because they love both parents, children cannot help being pulled in two directions when parents disagree. The distress in the children can be easily overlooked by both Mom and Dad, who may be overwhelmed by their own needs to survive.

Even more tragic—and quite common—is a child's erroneous acceptance of some responsibility or guilt for the family crisis. A son or daughter may worry, "Did Dad leave home because I was bad? I shouldn't have yelled at him when I was mad. I could have helped him more and done what he said. Maybe it's all my fault."

One young girl told a neighbor, "Daddy left home because I didn't behave." A small boy confided to his Sunday school teacher, "I'm a very bad boy. Daddy left us 'cause I didn't clean my room." Then with teary eyes he added plaintively, "I want my daddy back again!"

A high school freshman shared how she felt when her parents were divorced: "I was caught right in the middle. Because Mom and Dad refused to talk to each other, they passed their messages through me. I tried not to take sides, but it was an impossible situation. Not only was I torn between my two parents, but after a while I began to feel responsible for their splitting up.

I began to think, I shouldn't have fought with my sister so much. Maybe if I hadn't been born they'd have gotten along better."

Sometimes children have little opportunity to express their feelings or be heard by adults. While grieving that their family unit is no longer the same, a child often rides an emotional roller coaster that denies sleep at night and a sense of belonging during the day.

Although joint custody is becoming more common, the father is often the one who moves out. If that is the case, a daughter may conclude that any man she trusts might abandon her. The potential for general mistrust of males can easily grow.

Another problem is that, in their loss of male companionship, some daughters' loneliness may lead them to seek attention through demeaning relationships. "It's important to have a guy so I can feel loved," one junior high girl told a reporter for *Newsweek*. "It doesn't matter if he's ugly or disgusting, as long as he pays attention to me."[2]

If the father is the one to leave, the sons may have problems because of the lack of opportunity for bonding and identification with their male parent.

Justin, a withdrawn high school sophomore, resents his dilemma. "One of the post-divorce wounds I carry," he told me, "is from the battles between Mom's house and Dad's house. When I'm at Mom's house I'm supposed to hate Dad. When I'm at Dad's house, I'm supposed to hate Mom. When I have dinner with Dad, he might say, 'You remind me of your mother,' and I sense he's rejecting me. Mom does the same thing. When she sees parts of my dad in me, I feel she resents me because I'm like him."

Justin feels powerless to do anything about being put in the middle between two warring people, and he also feels rejected by the two most significant persons in his life. Psychologists say that problems from a poorly handled divorce often seriously affect children's mental health.

The following seven tips for divorcing or separating parents can minimize the trauma of confused and suffering children:

■ Assure each of the children in the family that a pending divorce is in no way their fault. While you may be separating from a spouse, you're not parting company with the children.

- Explain to the children about when they will be staying with Mom or Dad or when they will get to visit the non-custodial parent. In most cases, the children will now have two homes. Be specific; tell them which days (or weeks or months) they will be with each parent, and reassure them that both parents love them and will do their best to help everything go smoothly.
- Accept the fact that your children will feel bewildered and helpless. They will probably find it difficult to express their confusion and fears. Be available to listen attentively. When your child wishes to talk, treat every question seriously.
- Honestly share your feelings with your children. Admit to being frustrated, lonely, sad, angry, and afraid. Your candor will help your children to be more open about their feelings.
- Allow your children to grieve. If it's your sincere intent, assure each of them that you will not desert them, that you will continue to love and care for them.
- Realize that a child's healing process will be slow. Expect that each child may respond differently. Be tolerant of unique grief reactions and unusual behavior.
- Each child will need to be assured of God's unconditional love for him or her, as well as of your unconditional love.
- Pray with your children. Ask God for his healing presence as well as his guidance in your new family circumstances.

RECONCILING WITH THE PAST

Neither my dad nor I ever had an opportunity to sit down as adults and review our early relationship. Dad left his European home for the United States when he was seventeen. I was still a teenager when he died. Years after his death when I decided to visit my father's relatives near his birthplace on an outlying island in the Baltic Sea, I understood my father's role in our home from a new perspective.

Visiting his close relatives, I learned that the typical father's role was to be controlling and authoritarian. Once I realized that my dad was the target of intemperate child-rearing methods himself, it seemed only logical that Dad might parent me as he was parented.

Realizing this, my resentments began to mellow. Eventually I could say, "Dad, now I understand you as a bruised being I never knew before." I could accept that my dad had done his best, considering the parenting he experienced as a child. With relief, my stowaway child and I jettisoned much of the "grudge luggage" of resentment we had harbored for so many years. I thanked God for the peace-filled release that flows from the healing act of forgiveness.

INSIGHTS FOR PARENTS

1. Children who feel abused by an earthly parent often experience difficulty accepting the love of their heavenly Father.

2. The most important gift parents can give a child is consistent, unconditional love. Without that, young people may feel unwanted and endure an unhappy, insecure existence.

3. When older, a child who was abused may gravitate to an adult abuser. The unmet need for attention can be so great that the pain of regular abuse is preferable to being ignored.

4. Children who feel bewildered and neglected when their parents separate need regular opportunities to be heard, to ask questions, and to express their feelings.

5. In times of crisis, children need parents who stay calm and say, "I love you no matter what happens. We can pray and work through this together."

6. Each mom and dad needs to know and accept God's unconditional love. If we as parents love ourselves shabbily, that is also likely to be the way we love our children.

7. Parents who torment their children often do so because it provides adults with a natural outlet for aggressive feelings bottled up since childhood.

8. "If we could read the secret history of others, we would find in each person's life enough sorrow and suffering to disarm all our hostility."—Henry Wadsworth Longfellow

THINGS TO DO

You may review the following questions alone or use them for discussion in a parents' group.

A. When disciplining your child, do churning emotions and old feelings of rejection sometimes dominate your actions? Or are you able to impersonally make a clear distinction between the behavior that you're rejecting and the son or daughter you still love?

B. How many of us parents conceal feelings of personal inadequacy from our children by covering them with a facade of self-assurance? Are we aware that by doing so we're setting our children up for personal frustrations whenever they compare their inner feelings of low self-worth with the mask of success we project as a parent?

C. If you and your spouse have experienced considerable discord, separation, or divorce, have you been careful to avoid any perception of blame from falling on a child or children who may assume responsibility for the strife?

8

How Put-Downs
Harm Children

*Criticism is hard to take, especially from
a family member, a relative,
a friend, or a stranger.*

As a child, did you ever chant, "Sticks and stones may break my bones, but words will never hurt me"? That old canard is catchy but untrue. Chronic teasing and cruel nicknames can crush a youngster's self-concept.

TAUNTING AND TEASING

Unable to tolerate any more of a classmate's teasing, fourteen-year-old Ben pulled out a pistol and pointed it at the head of the girl who made him the object of her taunts. Pleading desperately with him not to shoot, Tanya fell to the floor and crawled slowly out of the room as the angry young man followed her to the door. Finally he fired three shots into the classroom walls before surrendering his weapon.

The assistant principal considered Ben a model student prior to this flare-up. A classmate explained that Ben "freaked out" because Tanya persisted in taunting him. Another student recalled that "she always called him 'rapper' because he wore a leather hat. She called him other names, too. But most of the time Tanya would just sit there and glare at him."[1]

Teasing always occurs at the victim's expense. A college student who suffered taunting as a child still remembers the agony. "How it hurt when they'd tease me," he said. "I couldn't forget the vicious things some of them said and then how the others all laughed. Their mockery crushed what little self-confidence I had."

A graduate student of mine cannot erase a childhood experience from his memory. "I was in an elementary school choral class," he began. "Day after day the teacher would frown, stop the singing and declare, 'Something is wrong with the pitch.' Then Miss Johnson would have some pupil sing a few notes. The day came when I was asked to sing part of a song. Elated, Miss Johnson proclaimed, 'I have found the problem at last.' Striding to the instrument cabinet, she pulled out a tambourine, marched over to me, stuck it in my hand and pointed me to the percussion section. My classmates burst into laughter. From then on they all called me 'Tambo.' I've never tried to sing with others again."

IN-FAMILY TEASING

Parents who laugh . . . at a child can mark that
child permanently, make him feel unloved.
Perhaps nothing of an ordinary nature can hurt
more . . . than laughter.
—Eugenia Price

My wife and I help support a child in Taiwan. While in Taipei, we arranged to visit Lin. She lived with her mother and six relatives in a small house. Lin's aunt hurried to school to bring her home.

On her arrival, Lin was confused when two Caucasian strangers wished to befriend her. Then one relative bent over the little girl and announced playfully, "These are your foster parents from America. They've come to take you home with them!" Everyone giggled. Such joking may amuse adults, but "fun" at the expense of a small child is devastating.

Suddenly frightened of Lois and me, Lin hid behind her mother. Any possibility of a friendly relationship with this special child had been lost. Adults may rationalize that such actions are "just good-natured banter," but who can claim that teasing a defenseless child is ever a loving act?

I was eighteen months old before I walked by myself. While physically able to walk, I was afraid to venture out on my own unless holding on to something. One day someone placed my security-seeking fingers around the side of my rompers. With that for assurance, I walked off by myself for the first time.

This episode became a favorite anecdote to share with guests in our home. Whenever a family member repeated the details for visitors, the punch line prompted hearty laughter. Yet as the butt of the banter, I never thought that incident was funny. I became convinced that there must be something peculiar about me to warrant such a reaction.

In her book *Toxic Parents*, Susan Forward tells about a father who made a pretext of studying his son carefully. Then he declared to his wife, "This boy can't be ours. Look at that face. I'll bet they switched babies on us in the hospital. Why don't we take him back and swap him for the right one?"[2]

Parents may consider such jesting "just good, clean fun," but children usually take exaggerations at face value. Years ago, Friedrich Nietzsche asserted that people do not kill by wrath as often as they do by laughter at the expense of a defenseless person.

Loving parents should discourage in-family teasing. We can also help our children by modeling constructive ways to react to taunts. They benefit from observing adults who don't take themselves too seriously and from noting our ability to laugh at ourselves and our foibles. It may help children to know that those who continually belittle others often feel inadequate about themselves. Whenever possible, encourage children to accept God's unconditional love for them as the foundation of their own self-worth.

NICKING AWAY WITH NICKNAMES

People can put up with rebukes
but they cannot bear being laughed at . . .
or appearing to be ridiculous.
—Molière

Nicknames make a tremendous impact on a child's sense of self-worth. Frequently the pain of such negative labeling will shrivel a youngster's self-esteem. Unfortunately, a child finds no adequate defense against a nickname.

While leading an adult seminar on self-worth, I asked members to recall and share positive, as well as hurtful, nicknames.

Negative labels tumbled out easily, but the group had difficulty identifying many positive descriptions.

Seminar participants classified the negative nicknames in three categories:

Physical	Social	Mental
Fatso	Motor-mouth	Knucklehead
Runt	Nosey	Dummy
Duck Feet	Klutz	Scatterbrain
Schnoz	Stinky	Stupid
Piano Legs	Loud Mouth	Idiot
Elephant Ears	Dingbat	Numbskull
Gopher Teeth	Clumsy	Dopey
Shrimp	Freak	Lamebrain
Buzzard Beak	Skinflint	Meathead

The group struggled to develop the following list of positive nicknames:

Pal	Princess	Sunshine
Light of My Life	Beloved	Sweetheart
Buddy	Dear One	Tiger

While endearing names are comforting, heartless nicknames isolate a child from his or her peers. One woman told me, "Nobody wanted to be my friend when everyone knew me as Fatso." William Hazlett wrote that "a nickname can be the hardest stone the devil can throw at an individual."

Parents who can justifiably claim, "I've never laid a finger on my child," may still have crushed the self-esteem of their youngsters with cruel nicknames.

EMOTIONALLY ABUSIVE REMARKS

The bruises from cruel words are internal and long-lasting.

A participant in my self-worth seminar confided that her own self-esteem was at the bottom of the scale. Rachel struggled to control her tears. "I've never admitted this to anyone before, but I've had dreadful difficulty believing in myself. What hurt most was the day my mother became disgusted with me and blurted, 'Oh, how I wish you'd never been born!' What in the world could I possibly do about that? Ever since that day, my inner stowaway child has been convinced that I'm unwanted by my own mother. At other times she'd insist, 'You'll never amount to anything.' I heard that so often there's no way I could avoid believing her."

Even the most well-meaning parent can slip into repeating negative remarks when trying to control a child. A speaker at a conference for parents told of a study of 150 girls aged nine to twelve who were asked what bugged them most about their mothers. Many volunteered the same answer, "Her screaming at me."

"Oh, oh! There's Mommy at the
scream door!"

Why do parents fall into such a habit? Because when we're at our wit's end, screaming is one of the few techniques that seem to get the desired reaction. It's difficult to give up something that works when so few things a parent stumbles across offer any predictable results.

Considering the number of teenagers living on the streets today, we're forced to ask, "What's going wrong in our homes?"

Emotional abuse by parents always demeans a child. Many youth are being regularly belittled at home by remarks like these:

- "You're pathetic. Can't you ever do anything right?"
- "You'll never amount to anything."
- "I guess I just can't trust you."
- "What did I do to deserve you?"
- "You're a bum and you'll always be a bum."
- "Someday you'll have kids just as rotten as you are."
- "Who'd want to marry a slob like you?"
- "You don't have any character or willpower."
- "You're so stupid I can't believe you're my child!"
- "You'll be the death of me yet!"

Have you ever said anything similar as an exasperated parent? Conversely, how often do you make appreciative and supportive comments to your children?

Parents may feel relieved that they never or rarely say such destructive things to their children, but they may not realize that they are using more subtle criticisms that are also harmful. Continual remarks about not doing things as well as expected, hints on how to improve, and corrections made for the child's "own good"—all those done frequently and unkindly can also shrink a child's self-esteem.

Few parents realize the lasting emotional impact of negative judgments placed on the supple minds and hearts of their children. Individual appraisals by a mom or dad can be, on one extreme, the source of untold misery or, on the other, of joy-filled memories extending into adulthood and continuing long after a parent's death.

FEELINGS OF SHAME

Peter Steinke, a counselor for a church social service organization in Texas, told a seminar group what he had found among his clients.

First, Steinke discovered that most of his clients are more troubled by shame than by guilt. Second, he found that the word *shame* appears in the Bible eight times more frequently than *guilt*.

Steinke explained that while guilt refers to what one has done, shame refers to who one is. Guilt pertains to a specific wrongdoing, but shame implies that one's whole self is faulty. As a result, part of the person in effect looks down on himself; the person who is shamed has been "found out" and feels exposed.

I heard a mother reproach her son after the Sunday morning service. "I was so *ashamed* of you in church today!" she fumed. Such broad-brush chastising is confusing to a child. It doesn't specify the cause of the mother's displeasure but leaves the boy to guess which faults he may have exposed that day. He could well interpret his mother's statement to mean, "As my child, you're really a big disappointment to me."

Steinke identified other self-judgments reached by those who are shamed:

- Scorned by my own parents, I'm just no good.
- I fear others will learn the truth about me. If that happens, I'll lose some friends.
- If I withdraw and stay by myself, others may not notice my faults.

Steinke concluded that parents who shame their children not only increase their children's dread of exposure but undermine their self-esteem.

NEGATIVE PROPHECIES

In a group discussion on self-worth for parents, Freda struggled with intense feelings while sharing a childhood experience. She told how she'd always wanted to snuggle in her mother's lap, yet she never experienced the security of that safe haven. Every time she attempted to climb up, her mother rebuffed her with "No, I can't hold you! You hurt my knees." Freda felt rejected and came to believe she was unlovable.

Thomas Gordon recorded the comments of a thirteen-year-old girl who was rebelling against her parents' standards.

"So often they tell me how bad I am, how I can't be trusted. . . . Now I actually do some half-baked things I know they won't like. If they're already convinced I'm bad and stupid, I might as well go ahead and do all these things they expect anyway."[3]

This daughter had insight. She understood the saying, "Tell a child often enough how bad she is and she will most certainly became bad." Parents should realize that their children may very well become what they tell them they are.

THE PITFALLS OF PERFECTIONISM

It's a continual challenge for adults with perfectionist tendencies to resist interfering with a child's responsibilities; for example, to keep their mouths shut when youngsters wrestle with a home or a school project. As the child works through a problem, parental reactions reveal Mom and Dad's level of trust and confidence in the child's problem-solving abilities.

Children from kindergarten through the fifth grade are at a stage in life when they enjoy being helpful. Often they'll seek opportunities to participate in a variety of responsibilities at home. This is a good opportunity to capitalize on their efforts with obvious delight and regular appreciation.

Yet the first time a child offers (or is asked) to set the table, is it reasonable to expect a flawless spread? How important is it if the cutlery is mispositioned? Is the mistake worth adding to a child's feeling of inadequacy? This doesn't mean that we won't teach a child the "right" way to do a task. Yet the correction should never overshadow a child's helping effort, discouraging the youngster from trying for fear of making a mistake.

Moms and dads who are perfectionists often demand a level of performance that dooms a child to disappointment and feelings of inferiority. The "Here, let me do it" tendency suggests an obsession with inerrancy that leads to put-downs of their children. Instead, parents need to accept a child's offer of help and the imperfect results with genuine appreciation. Improvements will come with more experience, age, and self-confidence.

It's not easy to allow a child to help you paint the picnic table without going over his work a second time to be certain all brush strokes are parallel; or to let her make her own bed without taking over by smoothing every wrinkle and refluffing the pillow; or to let the kids help decorate the Christmas tree and resist rearranging the ornaments to places you consider more appropriate.

The following are some recommendations for perfectionist parents.

- Give each child tasks within his general ability level.
- Avoid making a big issue of a child's blunder. Instead, gently and quietly help her to learn from the error.
- If your child makes a mistake, make a distinction between the individual and the act. You may be critical of the action, but still show your love for the child.
- Resist comparing the accomplishments of different children. Doing so is an obvious put-down that says, "You're inadequate when compared with others."
- Plan a "family foible sharing time." As Mom and Dad, be human enough to admit some of your prized goofs. Provide an opportunity for children to participate, but never force them to share or allow them to tell on a sibling.
- Emphasize that each child is assured of your unconditional love regardless of human imperfections.

INSIGHTS FOR PARENTS

1. Children have difficulty distinguishing parental joking from reality. They typically accept "humorous" adult exaggerations as the truth.

2. What we as parents thoughtlessly say, then quickly forget, our daughters and sons may carry inside for the rest of their lives.

3. An emotional outburst at a defenseless child is like squeezed toothpaste—it was easy to get it out but practically impossible to restore to its original situation.

4. Children bruised by a parent's verbal fault-finding learn to criticize and reject both themselves and others.

5. The act of shaming children not only tells them they are faulty creatures but also suggests that their God and their family will find them difficult to love.

6. Parents need to refuse to label a child with some nickname because it seems funny to them or to others. A child has no defense against such negative labels.

7. Humiliating a child may satisfy an adult's need to feel superior, but it crushes the youngster's self-confidence, replacing it with insecurities.

8. If we help our children realize they are God's unique creatures and fully accepted by God's infinite love, they will have a firm foundation for lifelong self-esteem.

THINGS TO DO

A. If you find it easy to tease a child, stop and think: Did you grow up in a home where taunting and teasing were considered "family fun"? If so, recall your reaction to that teasing as a child. How did it make you feel about yourself?

B. Reflect carefully and list for discussion the put-downs and negative comments children hear most frequently in your home, as well as supportive comments you'd like to use more often with your children.

9

Nurturing Family Members

The family is the most crucial ingredient in nurturing or neglecting a child's self-esteem.

—California Task Force to Promote Self-Esteem (1990)

Happy is the person whose memories of home are filled with nurturing affirmations of parental love. I have a friend who told me that one of his favorite childhood experiences was "Mother sitting on the edge of my bed telling me, 'Paul, your father and I love you very much. Every day we thank God you're part of our family.' Now, I find myself sharing similar feelings with our children."

How different our society would be if every child felt nourished at home. When parents fail here, young people are driven to seek love and acceptance elsewhere, often with heartbreaking consequences. Parents' attitudes and actions in the home either build or bruise a child's self-esteem.

CLEAR SIGNALS, AUTHENTIC MODELS

It's no good to have confidence in a child if we don't express it. The last thing a child needs is to wonder whether or not Mom or Dad believes in his potential and worth. Even worse is a disparaging statement such as, "I doubt that you'll ever amount to much." After all, do we as parents actually deserve God's mercy and grace? No. Which of us could survive if God labeled us "undependable" after we'd bungled a few times?

Being honest with each child is essential if parents want their children to be open with them. If parents won't admit to occasional self-doubts, their masks of perfection confuse children. Youngsters find it supportive and nurturing when moms and dads share some of their struggles, emotional strains, and failures. When children realize that such problems are a part of life, they are better prepared for their own blunders and occasional sags in self-esteem.

NO DEPOSIT, NO RETURN

Picture each child in your family as a love bank in which you make daily deposits and withdrawals. In every interaction with your child you either make a caring deposit or a careless withdrawal. Your goal in "love bank parenting" is to maintain a substantial surplus of love in each child's individual account.

Parents should never assume there is a favorable balance in a child's love account just because the number of deposits equals or exceeds the number of withdrawals. One emotion-laden, sarcastic comment can be traumatic enough to break the bank. It usually takes a number of substantial deposits to offset one careless withdrawal and ensure a favorable balance in your child's love bank.

THE WIN-WIN CONFLICT RESOLUTION STRATEGY

A family that knows how to nurture will nevertheless experience some problems. Knowing what to do when conflict arises can keep your relationships supportive and healthy.

Parent-child clashes often become power struggles in win-lose situations and nurturing goes out the window. In such unequal matches the parent usually wins because he or she has more physical and psychological strength. Children often feel powerless and resort to destructive ways to make their point and influence the outcome.

By contrast, in win-win problem solving, the child participates in a joint search for a solution that both parties can accept. When this is accomplished, heavy-handed authority becomes unnecessary. Advantages of the win-win conflict resolution strategy include the following:

- The child is invited to help find a solution.
- A higher-quality solution usually results when both parties participate.

- There is a natural motivation to accept the agreement.
- Opportunities arise for the parent to compliment the child for good thinking.
- Less need exists to resort to parental power.
- Children's self-understanding improves as they learn to express their inner feelings.
- Children learn an effective lifetime technique for dealing with difficulties.

THE SUCCESSFUL PROBLEM-SOLVING PROCESS

Parents can strengthen their children's self-esteem by including them in solving family problems. The following suggestions present an approach that helps resolve family difficulties. For this list I've drawn on Irv Goldaber's ideas presented in his "Win-Win" conflict resolution seminar as well as Thomas Gordon's thoughts concerning a "no-lose" program for raising children.[1]

1. As a parent, set aside the time required to sit with your child and together seek a solution that both can accept. As chapter five suggested, avoid accusing "you" messages. Instead, define how you feel about the problem with "I" messages. Listen attentively to your child's point of view. Stifle the temptation to interrupt with parental wisdom.

2. Before listing possible solutions, take your child's hand and ask God for guidance in the joint effort. Then suggest that a number of possible solutions exist. Encourage your child to share some suggestions first. At this early point in the process, don't evaluate or put down any idea. Add to the list as long as either of you has more ideas to volunteer.

3. Invite your child to indicate which of the options looks better to her. Frequently the child will recommend a solution that is fair to both. If that does not occur, state clearly in an "I" message why a choice does not seem adequate to you. Request that the child choose another alternative that might be acceptable.

4. When agreeing to a solution, avoid implying, "Now we have the final answer." Instead, recommend that both of you test the proposed solution for a week or so. If it works well, then adopt it. If it fails to satisfy, discuss some possible modifications or agree to test another alternative.

5. Once you have found a good solution, take time to celebrate. Praise your child for his good thinking and cooperation. Take your child's hand once more and join in a prayer of thanksgiving for God's guidance.

This method is particularly valuable if begun when a child is young. Don't expect every attempt to be 100 percent effective. Realize that the process used may be as important as the end product. Resist using your authority to subvert the plan for your personal advantage. When properly employed, this procedure will be a significant step toward family unity and harmony.

NURTURING SELF-CONFIDENCE

The best time to establish trusting relationships between parent and child is when the child is young. In a survey on the moral life of youth, Robert Coles found that 82 percent of elementary students would ask a parent for moral advice; only 53 percent of high school students said they would.[2]

To nurture your child's self-confidence:

- Give your child numerous opportunities to make choices. You build self-esteem by expressing confidence in the child's decision-making ability.
- Even if your child's choice is not an eminent success, search for something positive to recognize.
- Never hesitate to commend your child in public. When you need to reprimand, do so in private.
- When praising a child, comment on specific behaviors: "I appreciate the fact that you. . . ."
- Regardless of your individual interests, support the group activities in which your child participates.
- Make your child's friends feel welcome in your home.
- Create opportunities for your children to bond with their grandparents as often as possible.
- Set aside the time required to learn new things with your children. They'll get a boost in self-esteem when they do something better than their parents.

"Then what ELSE did mommy do when she was
a little girl?"

Moms and dads who strive to do their best may someday
be rewarded with a note of appreciation. One son wrote to his
parents:

> Thank you for the many times you said to us,
> "We have faith in you. Knowing you as we do, we're
> sure you'll always do fine." You gave us so much
> encouragement! Even if we did something wrong, you
> were confident we'd change and not do the same
> thing again. Thanks for taking time to chat with us
> and listen without prejudging us. And you always
> thought we were great, especially when we didn't
> believe in ourselves. We appreciate you both for
> being such understanding, supportive parents. We
> never doubted your love for us!

NURTURING IN BLENDED FAMILIES

An increasing number of adults are responsible for nurturing other people's children. This often occurs following a second

marriage. Adults select their new mates, but children have no equal opportunity to choose a stepparent or new siblings. The youngsters come as part of a package deal. In such new relationships siblings cannot be expected to love each other automatically. It should surprise no one if a child resists a new stepparent's expectations for behavior in the blended family. The following guidelines can help parents work together on their new responsibilities in a blended family:

- Go slowly. Developing good relationships will take time.
- Listen with your whole self. Say little. Attend carefully to what a child may be saying between the lines of conversation.
- Strive to understand what life must be like for the children, both your own and your spouse's. Neither may have been stepchildren before. Listen to them, talk with them. Let your attitude communicate to each one, "I care about you. Tell me what you are feeling."
- Always expect good behavior. Act surprised at any evidence of misbehavior. Avoid saddling a child with reminders of former misdeeds.
- Never ridicule or laugh at a child's ideas. Search for positive values in what the youngster has shared.
- Probe for overlooked areas of expertise or talent in each child. Once discovered, acknowledge that child as your "resident expert" in that specialty.
- Recognize each child's positive qualities and traits. Be particularly alert to this when focusing attention on a quiet, withdrawn child.

WIDER CIRCLES OF NURTURING

The only ones who will really be happy are those
who will have sought and found how to serve.

—Dr. Albert Schweitzer

"I'll never forget Julia Kinsel," said Dan Erlander, now chaplain at Pacific Lutheran University in Parkland, Washington. "She was a mentor for our youth choir. High school flooded us with countless expectations of things we had to do. Teachers pushed us to excel in classes and school activities. But Julia made no similar demands. She simply loved us with no preconditions. If we went to her with a problem, she took the time to listen and treat us with dignity and respect. Her love didn't depend on our grades or success in various activities. In her eyes we were worthwhile just as we were. For some young people in her choir, Julia's 'mother love' was the only adult affection they experienced."

This unusual teacher helped Dan and his classmates to understand that God's love is never erratic or conditional. In spite of all their imperfections and failures, her students sensed that they were accepted as new creatures in Christ. Julia made real for them the verse, "My grace is sufficient for you, for my power is made perfect in weakness" (2 Cor. 12:9 RSV).

A former student at Pacific University in Oregon, Howard Horner, recalled how boosting a kid's self-esteem at times might require little more than a few well-chosen words. His youth adviser at church, Marlene Andrews, said to him one day, "Have you considered going to Pacific University? I think the university would be good for you, and you'd be good for the university."

"That last comment bowled me over. I was only a raw farm kid," he said. "Just the idea of going to college was new in our family and scary for me."

Then one day in college Howard's literature professor, Dr. Stone, said, "Mr. Horner, I've never had a football player who earned an A in my Shakespeare class. Is it possible you might be the first?"

Again, a few carefully chosen words turned him on. Howard was overjoyed when his team tied for the league championship, but he was just as elated by the A he earned in Shakespeare.

"Now I wish at the time I had thanked Mrs. Andrews and Dr. Stone for their special interest and nurturing love at crucial times in my life," he says. "Their personal concern and thoughtfulness boosted my shaky self-confidence."

After college, Howard dedicated his life to helping other youth by serving as a caring teacher and later as an effective school administrator.

Knowing that other people in many settings will nurture our children is very comforting to us as parents, because we know we cannot meet all our children's needs. Thank God for providing so many people who know how to nurture and care enough to do so.

INSIGHTS FOR PARENTS

1. "Advice within the family is like snow; the softer it falls the longer it dwells and the deeper it sinks into the mind." — Samuel Taylor Coleridge

2. Each child's birthright should include the opportunity to spend quality time with parents. The amount of time that parents share reveals their level of commitment to nurture each child.

3. Parents should avoid qualifying their "I love you" statements to a child with any conditions such as "when you . . . ," "if you . . . ," or "as long as you. . . ."

4. Make as many deposits in your child's "love bank" as possible—and as few withdrawals as possible. Remember, one thoughtless, bruising reaction can bankrupt a child's love account.

5. "Affluenza," the indulging of youngsters with material possessions, will never substitute for the investment of real nurturing, that is, giving them your time, love, and personal attention.

6. Parents can check their nurturing practices with the following question: "When was the last time I put my arms around each of my children, looked them in the eye, and told them how much I love them?"

7. The inspiration of parents, teachers, youth group advisers, and other caregivers who live up to their faith is greater than the most convincing sermon.

A. Start each child's day on a positive note. Find something commendable you can recognize or celebrate, or offer some special expression of trust. Do this early in the day, preferably before the child leaves for school. You'll probably discover the day will go better for both of you.

B. Discuss with other parents some nurturing qualities you admire in their families. Select several positive traits you'd like to pass on to your children. Identify a "trait-for-this-week" that you'll seek to incorporate in your parenting practices.

C. Reflect on other caregivers who are important in your children's lives. Develop a list of each child's schoolteachers, Sunday school teachers, or youth advisers who deserve your note of appreciation. Share your sincere thanks for the interest and the time she or he gives your child.

10

Different Gifts,
All Accepted

*While God wants us to make use of our unique
gifts, he still accepts us as we are.*

Brad, a seventeen-year-old high school student, knew his parents expected him to become a basketball star and earn a college scholarship as his two older brothers had. On the day he was cut from the varsity basketball team, he went home and threw a $20,000 tantrum. During his outburst, he took a baseball bat and destroyed furniture, smashed lamps, shattered mirrors, and broke windows.

Trouble had been simmering for a long time. Brad felt the subtle goading of his parents until his head of steam exploded. Ignoring the fact that their son possessed different gifts and interests, Brad's parents expected him to match his brothers' exploits, not perceiving that their third son had other goals, other strengths.

Ambitions for a child to excel in areas of parental interest can force a young person into agonizing feelings of inadequacy. Some moms and dads unconsciously crave the recognition associated with a youngster's athletic prowess and push their offspring hard just so they can bask in their child's accomplishments.

Dr. Jon Hellstedt, head of the psychology department at the University of Massachusetts in Lowell, once asked 104 young ski racers what degree of parental expectation they experienced. The psychologist found that parents often see their children as more capable than the kids see themselves. As a result, many children experience excessive pressure and anxiety. Hellstedt also found that half the young racers reported their parents would be "very upset" should they withdraw from competitive skiing.

"The reason they can play that
good is their parents aren't
yelling at them from
the sidelines."

THE PAIN OF PARENTAL COMPARISON

Parents diminish their children when they compare them to others with different gifts. I once overheard a mother in a supermarket command her son to "Say hello to Mrs. Simpson." The small boy just stared at the floor. Displeased with his reaction, the mother explained, "Tim's nothing like his sociable sister. He's always been so shy!"

The second mother then labeled her youngsters by commenting, "In our family, Erin has always been the smart one. Derek here is the comedian. He's a real oddball."

Paul Tournier warns that "to put a label on someone is inevitably to contribute to making that individual conform to the label, especially if the person is at the impressionable age of childhood."[1]

Most children differ from their siblings in personality, motivation, intelligence, athletic ability, artistic talent, and mechanical skills. Not only is each child dissimilar, but siblings become increasingly diverse as they grow older.

Asking a child, "Why can't you be more like your sister (or brother)?" is thoughtless and demoralizing. It's about as reasonable as asking, "Why don't you have brown eyes like your brother . . . curly hair like your sister . . . twenty-twenty eyesight like our other children?" Sad to say, the message the youngster hears is, "You're not OK as you are."

THE MISERY OF BEING DIFFERENT

Kids like to dress the way their friends do. When comparing themselves with peers who parade the latest fads, they often feel inferior. Studying themselves in a mirror, they can always find some blemish, such as freckles, pimples, a large nose, protruding ears, teeth that are misaligned, or feet that are too big. It is typical for kids to judge themselves by external standards, always fearful of being different from their in-group's way of acting and dressing.

A highly regarded pastor surprised me by divulging how he felt about himself in high school. "I considered myself to be a social misfit," he began, "a dimwit, a blah. Socially I was 'dog-breath.' As an adolescent I felt I wasn't worth anything."

Another friend I admire has served as a dedicated, effective educator. (Often I wished my children had been under his guidance.) Recently he volunteered that "intense feelings of worthlessness have hovered over me from childhood to this very minute. It will sound strange, but I tried not to be like my dad. He always described himself as a failure. He'd admonish me, 'Son, don't turn out like your old man.' My mom countered with, 'Your dad is a wonderful man, so kind and loving.' Yet as I saw it, Mom left out those seemingly important male qualities of being strong and decisive. That's probably why I joined the Marines as soon as I was old enough to enlist."

After his military service my friend worked "in less competitive positions than many of my peers. Though I was fairly successful, relentless feelings of comparative worthlessness still live inside me, even as I write this letter. I'm plagued with feelings of, 'Why wasn't I able to succeed in more impressive positions like my friends?' The little success I've had isn't nearly enough to overcome my inner child's nagging feelings of inadequacy, my conviction that I'm worth less than others. All my life I've suffered with a bush league self-concept, beginning with my feelings of self-rejection as a small child at home."

GOD'S GIFTS OPEN DOORS

The gifts we possess differ as they are allotted
to us by God's grace, and must be exercised
accordingly.
—Romans 12:6 (NEB)

No child is ever bypassed when God hands out gifts and abilities, yet many either overlook or downgrade the talents received. It's easy to wonder, "Why did God give me *this* talent when I'd much prefer those my best friend has?"

James McNeill Whistler's testimony illustrates this dilemma. Wishing for a military career, he was elated to be admitted to West Point. Later, however, he flunked a class and had to drop out. After adjusting to this crisis, Whistler began to develop his artistic ability and became famous as a painter.

Children need to hear about adults who have experienced God's reorientation toward gifts they previously had ignored or failed to recognize. Both young people and adults must realize that the disappointment of a closing door in one vocational area may prove to be a blessing in disguise, one that eventually guides them to another door opening on a more fitting vocational alternative.

The Apostle Paul lists a variety of gifts that God gives to people. In Romans 12:6-8 and 1 Corinthinians 12:4-31, he mentions many, including administration, teaching, speech, charity, leadership, and service to others. All are valuable and all come from God. Parent-child discussions that examine the wide range of vocational opportunities open to youth are most helpful. These are particularly important to a brother or sister who covets a sibling's talent. Happy families not only recognize but celebrate the range of dissimilar gifts found in their members. Discussions on the importance and the satisfaction of Christian service can help young people consider the possibility of a life dedicated to serving others.

GIVE YOUNG PEOPLE TASKS THAT STRETCH

In spite of what they know about the variety of gifts God bestows on people, some adults in our congregations tend to ignore or depreciate the significant talents young people possess. They do this by:

- embracing the erroneous notion that today's young people are indifferent, apathetic individuals unwilling to become involved in service to people in need,
- accepting the passé but lingering philosophy that children should be seen but not heard,
- failing to question the fallacy that children have multiple rights but few responsibilities, and
- neglecting to challenge church youth with opportunities for significant service.

To many adults, the only service suitable for young people in the congregation involves such simple chores as collecting, sorting, and bundling old newspapers. Those are not demeaning service functions, but what do repetitious tasks say about our level of trust and confidence in the abilities, gifts, and talents of tomorrow's leaders? How are we nurturing them if we don't see them as having real gifts to offer others?

I rejoiced when I learned of a congregation where high school youth regularly staff a telephone hot-line to help neighborhood adolescents in need of peer counseling. Other youth in the same church direct an after-school tutoring program for children who need help with their homework. Younger children in the church are not excluded from community service. Some visit veterans' hospitals and nursing homes; junior high youth assist in the church nursery. Smaller churches can participate in one or more of these programs either alone or in cooperation with other congregations in their area.

In some congregations young people handle portions of a Sunday service once a month. In others, youth periodically have responsibility for an entire Sunday service. Most adolescents like being trusted. They grow when allowed to assume responsibilities.

When I served as a high school principal, I became convinced that when adults trust adolescents with appropriate responsibilities, young people handle their tasks as well as many adults. If some of their efforts misfire, we can help them analyze what went wrong and what changes might correct the situation. It's irrational to mistrust all young people because a few fail. How much better to demonstrate genuine trust in our children!

INSIGHTS FOR PARENTS

---

1. Unfortunately, parents sometimes worry that a child's low performance in school reflects poorly on them. Such concerns often result in placing unreasonable demands on the child to excel mainly to bolster a parent's esteem.

2. Guide your children to avoid downgrading themselves by comparisons with more capable friends. Youngsters who see themselves as incompetent tend to become the label they've assumed.

3. We can remind our children of Paul's wisdom: "Examine your own conduct for yourself; then you can measure your achievement by comparing yourself with yourself, not with anyone else" (Galatians 6:5, NEB).

4. Parents who are unsure of themselves may pretend to be unshakably confident. This confuses their children, who see themselves as inadequate by comparison.

5. It's exhausting for both children and adults to wear a mask in order to appear to be someone greater than they are. On the other hand, our self-esteem gets a boost when we are our true selves and find that others accept us as we are.

6. Genuine self-worth for youngsters is a gift from God. It does not depend on individual accomplishment. We all have immeasurable worth in God's eyes.

7. Parents can delight in God's creative handiwork in each of their family members, thank God for granting each one unique gifts, and see their children as having talents yet to be discovered and utilized.

8. A prayer for parents and children:

> ***Lord, if I am unique,***
> ***different from any before or ever to come,***
> ***then take away my competitive spirit,***
> ***and any war against others,***
> ***for they, too, are unique.***
> ***—Herb Brokering***[2]

THINGS TO DO

Discuss these topics with your spouse or with other parents.

A. Be honest. Are your special aspirations for a child at all similar to a dream you had for yourself when you were young? Is such an imposed ambition fair or realistic, considering that each person has different interests and gifts?

B. Listen carefully after you ask each child about his or her lifetime interests and goals. Recognizing that children's goals may change through the years, repeat this discussion with them as needed. Display personal interest and accept each child's current goal without attempting to "sell" your own preferences.

C. Commend your children whenever they attempt to explore their special gifts and develop their individual talents. Emphasize that it's perfectly acceptable to enjoy our special aptitudes, even though they may differ from the interests of others in the family or of our friends.

II

Trying to Earn
Acceptance and Love

*For by grace you have been saved through
faith, and this is not your own doing;
it is the gift of God—not the result of works,
so that no one may boast.*
—Ephesians 2:8-9

At twenty-nine, Euleta Usrey was a brainy college graduate who had just been promoted to the position of department head in a major company. She was engaged to be married. From all appearances, life was sweet for this enviable young woman. And yet the morning came when a suicide note was found beside her bed. It read: "Only death will suffice to extinguish my pain."

What pain? Life was beautiful for Euleta Usrey.

By the time medics arrived, Euleta had stopped breathing. They rushed her to the hospital, where she was ultimately revived and nursed back to health. While convalescing, the young woman admitted to her weeping mother that she had been considering killing herself since she was a little girl.

"You can't *mean* that!" her mother gasped. "You're the most successful young person I know. You're number one in everything you do. I've always been so proud of you."

Euleta shook her head sadly. "That was the only reason I was number one—so you'd be proud of me and love me. I knew that if I ever failed, then. . . ." She stared at the floor and began to sob.

Suddenly her mother realized that her family's major message to Euleta had always been, "Work hard! Compete! Succeed!" Euleta's mother had even taken courses in child psychology to learn all she could about motivation. Yet she couldn't recall any of those books advising that parental love should be independent of a child's success or failure, a gift and not something to be earned.

Though Euleta had left home years before this, her anxious inner child was still emotionally dependent on earning her mother's approval.[1]

WANTING OUR CHILDREN TO BE EXCEPTIONAL

Parents who are determined to raise model children force their kids to struggle against fantastic odds. No matter how ardently a child strives to please those eager parents, no one can ever measure up to all of these parental aspirations. The expectations piled on children like Euleta often result in such a compulsion for perfection that nothing is good enough. The high cost of attempting to please everybody sets a child on a course that leads to stress, disappointment, and ultimately failure. These kids strive to become *self*-reliant, not *God*-reliant.

Euleta was not alone in her misery. Kim is a Chinese-American daughter who also heard the drumbeat of her mother's constant pushing to do better. Her persistent question to Kim was, "Why can't you be the top student in every one of your classes?"

These excessive demands caused Kim to become upset with herself at the slightest mistake. As her mother continued to compare her with the most capable students in school, Kim grew more restless and miserable. The "perfect" student and daughter her mother had set out to create turned into an obsessive-compulsive individual for whom life was a great burden and the future bleak.

SEEKING APPROVAL THROUGH HARD WORK

I understand some of the struggles of Euleta and Kim. As a child I wrestled with a shabby sense of self-esteem. Because my older sister always brought home the highest grades possible, parental pressures landed on me to equal her achievements. Unable to match her record, I tried to compensate with a combination of perseverance and perfectionism in my out-of-school jobs. I hoped to earn my parents' acceptance and approval by faithful and diligent work.

Many young people grow up feeling rejected because they are unable to measure up to their parents' expectations. They see themselves as failures. Sadly, criticized children don't stop to question the justice of their parents' expectations. They learn instead to doubt their own worth.

FLAWED BUT STILL ACCEPTABLE

Some who pursue perfection might appear to have achieved that goal, but they can't deceive themselves. Euleta, for example, though eminently successful, continually experienced turmoil behind her mask of self-confidence. For many years she had papered over her inner feelings of self-doubt and inadequacy. Regardless of how many accomplishments she could list on her résumé, she drove herself with the admonition, "I should be able to do better."

Kim bought into her mother's premise that she should be at the head of every class. The results of her striving contributed not to peace and well-being but to frustration and eventually a complete collapse.

Parents strengthen their children not by holding themselves up as examples to emulate but by admitting that they, too, are fragile, flawed human beings. For their own emotional health, children need to understand that parents also are fallible. Feigned parental perfection will confuse and alienate young people. Children are likely to picture God as yet another critical and demanding parent whom they will fear instead of loving and trusting. How can children accept unconditional love from a person they fear? We must teach them that God loves them and accepts them, no matter what their flaws or imperfections are.

WHEN OUR CHILDREN ARE LIKE US

Frequently a child reveals traits similar to those of one of the parents. At times we may find ourselves instinctively critical and impatient with a child. Why? With no malice, the youngster is simply displaying an inherited characteristic we dislike in ourselves—one we have struggled for many years to overcome. In such situations parents unknowingly tend to be as hard on their children as they are on themselves. In such a case, the child is powerless to earn our acceptance. We need to ask, "Am I touchy about my child's action because I reject a similar behavioral trait in myself?"

Today I realize that a number of my mannerisms undoubtedly aggravated my dad. I'm convinced that I unwittingly reminded him of some qualities in himself that he disliked. The combination of a parent's short fuse and a child's innocent mimicking of an undesirable trait are likely to lead to a negative reaction, one that is an emotional response rather than an analysis of motives.

In such situations, children may wonder why they have a difficult time earning our acceptance. Until we see what we are doing and stop, their self-esteem can suffer.

STRUGGLING TO EARN GOD'S BLESSING

In his congregation's newsletter, Pastor Dick Foege observed that "a lot of people who have been exposed to the Gospel are still bent on 'doing' something to earn their salvation. The reality that God accepts us in spite of our sinful and unacceptable selves is an issue of eternal importance. Yet it seems to evade us in our arrogant insistence that what we parents are or do is more important than what God has done.

"I'm not against good works . . . but they're meant to be the result of the Gospel, not the law. There is no commendable action of ours—no matter how worthy—which can affect our salvation. Children and young people must clearly understand from their parents that today's big lie is a reliance on 'works righteousness.' It's so appealing. It brings us such a sense of accomplishment, even self-righteousness. Yet grace is the truth, a certainty that invites a loving response from each of us."

It's normal for parents to want each child to be an exemplary, praiseworthy individual. Yet we may mislead our children by our actions. They may think that they also must struggle to qualify for God's love. Some of them may come to the conclusion that "only if I work hard enough will I be able to earn God's blessing." Thus they may project our conditional, provisional love unto God who loves them unconditionally.

REFUSING GIFTS OUT OF PRIDE

Human pride says there is no such thing as a free lunch. It's natural to want to be self-sufficient, to earn everything we get.

This kind of distorted thinking almost denied a dying father and his two sons a trip to Disneyland.

In Pastor Ed Markquart's congregation, a forty-three-year-old dad named Drew was a member of the University of Washington's police force when he became terminally ill. His friend, Lt. Randy Stegmeier, together with other co-workers, decided to take up an offering to give Drew and his sons a trip to Disneyland in Anaheim, California. The gift was finally accepted, but not without a lot of persuasion on the part of the benefactors.

At Drew's funeral, Lt. Stegmeier told the story of the reluctant father:

"When I went to give Drew the trip to Disneyland, the trip you officers gave, he wouldn't take it. 'It's free,' I said. 'It's free.' No, Drew wouldn't take it. Too much pride. Gotta pay your own way. Gotta earn it. But finally I persuaded Drew that responsible men also know how to receive gifts . . . freely given. It took Drew awhile to accept this free gift, but he did. Later I talked with Drew about the free gift of eternal life in Christ.

" 'Eternal life is a free gift, Drew,' I said. 'Freely given from God. Can't earn it. Can't buy it. It's totally free, like the trip the police force gave you to Disneyland. It's yours to accept, freely given.' Gradually Drew came to understand that and accept the free gift of eternal life."[2]

That's what all children and young people must understand about their self-worth. They can't earn it . . . can't buy it. . . . It's totally free.

"IT'S MORE BLESSED TO GIVE"

A first lesson for children is to realize that love from God and from their parents is freely given; there are no requirements about having to earn it. A second lesson is to be willing to *receive* God's love, their parents' love and gifts, and love and gifts from others. A third lesson, one that is sometimes forgotten in our culture, is to be able to *give*.

Sometimes it seems that most children think it's more blessed to *get* than to *give*. As parents we enjoy giving, but we may have overlooked teaching our children that same joy; we may have neglected to create opportunities for them to give. We can encourage our children to choose, wrap, and give away small gifts to others—friends, grandparents, each other. At Christmas we can help our children buy toys for programs that distribute gifts to children who otherwise might not get any.

An adult's attitude when receiving a gift from a child can have a powerful effect on the child's attitude toward giving. When you are a recipient of a gift, accept it with affection and enthusiasm. Use it with joy as soon as possible. Show your pleasure and genuine appreciation. Be sure that your children have a good time giving so they will learn to experience the blessings of sharing.

Children benefit from giving service to others in the community as well as in the home. These opportunities allow them to develop their unique gifts.

In an article titled "And a Little Child Shall Lead Them," Mark Cutshall writes about taking children to visit the elderly in rest homes to bring them happiness.[3]

"There's something about children that brings to the elderly new life and enthusiasm," he writes. "One 89-year-old widow commented, 'The little children get on my lap and hug me. I just love them. It's greater than being a millionaire!' Another lady said, 'I have eleven grandchildren, but I don't see my own as often as these special kids. How I love them.' "

Cutshall maintains that children as young as two years can engage in such ministries. Through personal involvement they learn a priceless lifelong lesson: It's truly more blessed to give than to receive.

INSIGHTS FOR PARENTS

---

1. Parents can share the Apostle Paul's counsel with the young people in their family: "For by grace you have been saved through faith; and this is not your own doing, it is a gift of God . . ." (Ephesians 2:8-9, RSV).

2. Parents with low self-esteem sometimes seek greater personal satisfactions by goading their children to excel.

3. Children with low self-esteem frequently develop into "pleasers." They often will do almost anything to earn another's acceptance.

4. Saddling a child with unrealistic expectations often becomes an unintended form of abuse since a child seldom questions parental expectations.

5. Many parents find it difficult to accept help from others. Their children may have the same problem and need to find out that accepting assistance can be a blessing that those who receive can give to those who help them.

6. "Few things help a child . . . more than to place responsibility on him, and let him know you trust him."—Booker T. Washington

7. There will be poor parents, better parents, and good parents. There will never be perfect human parents. Yet each of us can remind ourselves that we are accepted and loved in God's sight, and communicate that same love of God to our children.

THINGS TO DO

Review these topics for yourself or discuss them with other parents.

A. Think about your children and which of them you may discipline or correct more frequently. Ask yourself these questions:

"Is one child in our family more like me? Is one more like my spouse? Is one truly an original?"

"Am I prone to automatically rebuke the child most like me whenever his or her attitudes or actions remind me of traits I dislike in myself?"

"Do I unconsciously tend to favor or to criticize the child most like my spouse?"

Such an analysis could reveal why some child(ren) may have a difficult time trying to earn a parent's acceptance and building good self-esteem.

B. Discuss how parents can best keep up-to-date on each child's recreational and vocational interests. Review what you can do to provide opportunities for exploration of each child's current ambitions, even though they may not be consistent with your preferences.

12

The Power of Touch

*"[Jesus] stretched out his hand
and touched him. . . ."*

—Matthew 8:3

A number of years ago, infants in foundling homes would often die for no apparent medical reasons. Researchers found that even small children in orphanages wasted away from an illness known as marasmus—a gradual loss of flesh and strength from no discernible cause.

Concerned about this phenomenon, Dr. Rene Spitz took it upon herself to study the problem. She found that most infants in foundling homes had adequate medical care, good food, and clean cribs. But she discovered a common denominator in the troubled institutions: overworked employees had no time to hold, cuddle, and talk to the babies as their mothers would have. From a lack of touch, one in three of these babies died before their first birthday.

Dr. Spitz's research team hit upon an idea. They recommended bringing in additional women to hold, rock, and talk to the infants. The provision of this missing human contact resulted in a dramatic drop in infant mortality.

More recently, Dr. Steven Ringer, director of newborn services at Brigham and Women's Hospital in Boston, entered into an experiment he called "Kangaroo Care" for infants born prematurely. Instead of isolating preemies in an incubator behind thick plastic walls, he directed that hospitals add hands-on treatment to provide bonding between parents and child. This was accomplished by allowing the infant to lie in bed skin-to-skin on the chest of one of its parents. As a result, the medical staff charted fewer breathing problems, less energy-waste by fidgeting, more rapid weight gain, and a more constant body temperature among the infants.[1]

Given what was learned from these studies, volunteers are now visiting hospitals to serve as "cuddlers." They provide the essential human contact for premature babies and for ailing babies whose parents for some reason cannot visit the hospital frequently enough to satisfy their infants' need for the love associated with parental touch. Can you imagine a more satisfying service than this?

OUR HIGH-TECH, LOW-TOUCH WORLD

The touch factor varies greatly in different societies. In Anglo-American communities, boys grow up touching each other less frequently than do girls. Yet observers in the waiting rooms of veterinary clinics find no difference in the amount or frequency with which girls and boys touch their companion pets.

Sidney Jourad undertook a study to observe couples in restaurants and cafes all over the world. His quest was to record the number of times couples touched in the course of an hour. In London the average number of touches was slightly less than one. In Paris the average number was 110 touches. In Gainesville, Florida, the norm was two touches, while in San Juan, Puerto Rico, couples touched as many as 180 times an hour.

In societies where touching is common, men and boys often embrace each other and hold hands in casual, unconscious ways. In comparison, Anglo-American boys are touch-deprived.

As a kid, I was concerned that touching others could become embarrassing. My mother was affectionate, but my father's reserve and social distancing prevailed. A display of emotion was inconsistent with his boys-don't-cry philosophy. With a built-in uneasiness about touching other people, I needed many years to overcome my inhibitions.

TEACHERS WHO CARE

Elementary teacher Will Hayes was an outstanding instructor, even though well past retirement age. He had no fear of touching his students. When asked how he approached his sixth graders, Hayes listed his three objectives:

First: Caring. "You don't teach a class—you teach individuals," he said. "I get to know and care for every student."

Second: Self-worth. Will recognized the need each youngster has for self-esteem. "No matter what subject you teach," he said, "if kids don't feel good about themselves, they can't be whole persons."

Third: Touch. Touch can be an expression of the teacher's caring love. "I touch every child every day—pat a head, tweak an ear. I also tell my students how good they are—and that I love them. I have no qualms about using the word love, and I tell parents that."[2]

In the book *Home Remedies*, Gary Smalley tells of his daughter, Kari, who teaches second graders in an inner-city public school. Before becoming a teacher she decided that not a single child would leave her classroom at the end of a day without getting a hug, a touch, or some special encouragement. Like Will Hayes, her daily goal was to have both her actions and her words communicate that each child was precious and valuable.[3]

A study at UCLA supports the goal of these two teachers who are determined to keep "in touch" with their students. It found that everyone needs eight to ten meaningful touches a day to maintain good emotional and physical health.

JESUS, EXEMPLAR OF TENDER TOUCH

The touch of Jesus was a tangible, cherishing expression of love. Most of us are familiar with his parables, yet we're apt to overlook his nonverbal communication and its relationship to his concern for other people. Even when speaking, Jesus would reach out his hands to bless those near him. He would touch the little children, the lame, the blind, the lepers. Jesus also showed his love for little children by enfolding them in his arms.

When words seem to be inadequate and you want to show your children how much you cherish them, reach out and enfold them in your arms. This will help convince them of their importance to you.

HUGGING, AN ASSURING TYPE OF TOUCH

A hug is a perfect gift because
one size fits all and
nobody minds if you give it back.
—Anonymous

Hugs within the family circle were not a part of my background. Even as an adult I worried for years that others might misunderstand if I gave them a hug. Still, I sensed that I was missing a positive, meaningful experience.

If you had observed my early hugging attempts as an adult, you would have seen a cautious neophyte. The recipient of my hug, with whom I connected at shoulder level, must have sensed the wary formality of a novice hugger. Sometimes I'd add a nervous pat on the back, almost as if attempting to burp my partner. Slowly my confidence grew and I became a more upright hugger. Today I'm thankful for the patience and acceptance of numerous hug-mentors who helped me to mature in this important "ministry."

Tony, an eighty-year-old African American farm laborer, was one of my more memorable hug tutors. He was a giant of a man with a minimum of this world's goods. My wife Lois and I stopped at his home one Thanksgiving to share our greetings, to visit for a while, and then to leave some food and clothing. Though he had little to share, Tony had invited two other migrant laborers to his place for a Thanksgiving meal. As my wife and I were leaving, Tony wrapped his big arms around me in a bear hug. Looking me squarely in the eye, he boomed, "Ain't the Lord been good to us?"

What a powerful message his embrace bestowed in contrast to simply mouthing a few worn phrases like, "Thanks for stopping by."

Every child needs the security of healthful touches and affectionate hugs. With a welcoming smile we can lovingly enfold a child in the warm haven of a hug. We may choose to sing a familiar song or hum a tune while the child cuddles next to us or sits in our lap. When the session ends, we can give the child an extra tight hug as a final seal of approval. The experience of being cuddled against a mother's breast and of being hugged by a father

"This is my favorite place—
inside your hug."

will convey feelings of family affection like nothing else in the world.

Such endearment is welcome at any time, but it's especially important after parents find it necessary to reprimand a child. Some parents I know have adopted the practice of offering a "healing hug" after any disciplining of a child. It's also well to distinguish between the child's actions that you disapprove and the child whom you still love.

Do healing hugs apply also to teenagers? These kids have outgrown our laps but they'll never outgrow their need for healthful parental contact. Don't give up your favorite forms of contact, whether they be an arm around the shoulder, hugs, back-rubs, foot-massages, hand holding, or simply pats on the back. Psychologists find that if adults fail to touch teenagers in healthy ways, young people are more likely to seek touching experiences from anyone who will befriend them.

A colleague of mine encourages healthful hugs by distributing free hug coupons that read "Good for a hug or two from any cooperating individual." He gives them freely to family and friends. They're a gentle hint to share God's love through a healthful human touch.

SELFISH TOUCH

It's regrettable that something as positive and beautiful as touching can sometimes be exploitative. Studies by family therapists report that as many as one in four children may have been sexually mistreated by the time they are eighteen years old. Often the abuser is not a stranger but someone the child knows and possibly trusts.

What should parents do if a child suggests that he or she has been molested? First, it is essential to take the child seriously. Listen calmly without overreacting. Respect the rate at which the child wishes to share information. Offer support by assuring your child's safety while you arrange for help. Realize that your child is an undeserving victim and be sure to treat him or her as both normal and blameless.

Several other factors are important. When there are two parents in the home, they should agree on their approach to the problem. Discordant parental attitudes will only confuse the child further. It's also important to determine the facts as promptly as possible. The greater the times between the initial reporting of the incident, the interim investigation, and the conclusion, the greater is the possibility for a story to balloon in a small child's imagination. It is advisable for parents to seek helpful referrals through a church-related family service organization, a community crisis center, or a local school counselor.

ANIMALS AS TOUCH SPECIALISTS

Children in rural areas have more opportunities to enjoy the companionship of animals than do kids in urban areas. Our grandchildren who live on a farm delight in a variety of animal companions—cats, dogs, rabbits, sheep, cattle, and horses. Studies tell us that the companionship of a pet is often beneficial to individuals of any age.

Psychologists report that lonely youngsters react to a pet as though it were a sibling. In fact, a child often turns to a pet for solace after a sad, angry, or fearful experience. Companion animals are particularly congenial. They ask no questions, express no criticism.

Children with disabilities have often made remarkable improvements when given an opportunity to bond with an animal. Charlotte, a youth group leader, told me that her science club attracted many children who were insecure. She decided to use animal pets to help liberate her young charges from their painful shyness and diffidence.

Little Anna, a social isolate in her group, became friendly with Nosey, a pet hamster. Soon Anna was coming to Charlotte's house on a regular schedule to feed Nosey. She'd spend as much time there as possible, holding and chatting with the hamster. Several months later, Anna's mother thanked Charlotte for helping her daughter begin to move away from her painful aloofness toward her peers. The women agreed that the result of Anna's visits with Nosey had been close to miraculous. The hamster's companionship had a good effect on Anna's self-esteem as well as on her ability to talk with others.

Dr. Leo Bustad, dean emeritus of veterinary medicine at Washington State University, helped to organize the International People-Pet-Partnership Project. For many years he has studied the human-animal bond. When asked why animal pets are so special as companions, he gave the following reasons:

- Both children and adults touch animal pets almost unconsciously.
- Companion pets seldom avoid humans—their quiet, accepting presence comforts both children and adults.
- Animal pets treat every person who seeks them out as number one in their lives.
- The presence of a nurturing animal companion eases a child's or an adult's emotional stress.

PETS AS THERAPY FOR CHILDREN

In New York City's foster child program, Yvonne Gonski worked with girls who experienced multiple rejections while still

"I like dogs 'cause if you're doing
something stupid they don't yell
at you. They do it with you."

very young. Most of the young people were withdrawn, depressed, and hostile. They felt incapable of establishing any trusting relationships. Finally, Gonski used dogs as companions to improve the communication level of the emotionally disabled girls.

After several sessions with the dogs present, Gonski noticed significant improvement in the girls' behavior at school as well as in their foster homes. They were more relaxed and better able to articulate their feelings to the people who worked with them. Such results are consistent with other studies that show a slower heartbeat when an individual is in touch with either human friends or companion animals.

WHEN TOUCH SAYS IT ALL

Wilbur and I had been classmates in college. Although he was blind, his hearing and memory were so keen that he confidently walked around our campus without a cane. He was the most mobile sightless person I have ever known.

Recently I attended Wilbur's funeral. His wife, Loreen, is also blind, as were many friends in attendance. Watching them share their grief, I quickly realized how indispensable touch is to their communication. Sightless friends held each other's hands and patted each other's backs. Frequently one would press a cheek against another's face. In one compassionate act, another blind woman sympathetically cupped Loreen's face in two upturned hands. Feeling tears on the widow's cheeks, she tenderly wiped them away. Talking wasn't disparaged, but that laying on of hands was one of the most expressive evidences of caring I have seen. Words could never arouse the same depth of concern. Loreen's friends' gentle touching said it all.

Have you touched someone today?

INSIGHTS FOR PARENTS

1. Words are frequently inadequate to express the depth of feeling or concern that a touch or hug can convey.

2. Caring touch is as natural as breathing and almost as indispensable. If not cuddled and talked to, infants, children, and the elderly will suffer emotional malnutrition.

3. Youngsters and adults who get eight to ten meaningful touches a day are known to maintain better emotional and physical health.

4. Jesus shared his love with children and with the sick through his gentle touches. We can represent God's loving hands and enfolding arms to the discouraged, the hurting, and the lonely.

5. In many hospitals today, therapeutic touch is used to help relieve depression, anxiety, and pain. It is also known to bolster a patient's will to live.

6. A lonely child naturally turns to a pet when needing to talk about a sad, angry, or fearful experience.

7. The companionship of pets can actually boost a child's emotional health and self-esteem. Pets are completely loyal. They ask no questions, pass no judgments.

8. Recognize the power for good that God places in your hands. Use this gift by reaching out to children in touching love. Hold the hands of God's loved ones who may be emotionally, physically, or spiritually distressed.

9. A hug is a perfect gift—one size fits all; and nobody cares if you give it back.

THINGS TO DO

Use these suggestions alone, with your spouse, or with other parents.

A. Review your family's attitudes when you were a child in regard to positive touch. Has touching others been a natural or an unnatural reaction for you?

B. If you were touch-deprived as a child, arrange for some discussions with several other parents. Compare your childhood backgrounds. Share helpful suggestions for all to consider. Meet again in several weeks when each can report on progress or problems and benefits from the suggestions of others.

C. In the meantime, be particularly alert for in-home touch opportunities, such as occasions for celebration as well as times when a child feels disappointed or rejected. Lose no natural opportunity to serve as a family "hug therapist." Resolve that when you feel lonely or hurt, you will ask for a healing hug from your spouse or your children.

13

The Need for Forgiveness

*A life that needs forgiveness has
as its first duty to forgive.*

—Edward Bulwer-Lytton

t's been a tough day at work. You are supertired tonight—
somewhere between dog-tired and drained. When you open
the front door, you are assaulted by two perpetual-motion
minds and mouths. Your kids have launched a coordinated attack
on your opposition to their attending Jessica's all-night party. Be-
sieging you when you're so exhausted doesn't seem fair! Already
stressed, something inside you snaps and you blow up at your
daughters. Soon they are in tears and you wish that you had never
blasted away at them. If only you had set some limits and said,
"Not now, girls, I'm going to my time-out room for a few minutes
of rest and relaxation. We can talk about this after dinner."

FORGIVENESS AND LIMITS

In such a situation, parents may later ask forgiveness of
their children for exploding, but also suggest that the children ask
for forgiveness as well for not being very thoughtful. Families thrive
when all members are willing to forgive and accept each other in
spite of mistakes and faulty judgments.

We need to remember, though, that forgiveness and limits
work together. Parents want to model forgiveness for their children, yet chaos would result if no limits were set on some kinds
of behaviors. Children catch on quickly and might continue destructive actions if not stopped. If they are blandly forgiven with
no further questions even though they keep stealing money from

your purse or wallet, for example, they are likely to continue stealing.

When accidents, intentional harm, and misbehaviors occur, parents and children have to talk about them and find ways to deal with them. When a child expresses sorrow for a misdeed, parents could do great harm by withholding forgiveness. How tragic to miss an opportunity to model God's forgiveness to the child.

In some cases a second step is needed. If a negative behavior keeps recurring, parents need to set clear limits: "We love you, Jacob, but you cannot play with Daddy's computer when he isn't home. You have to stop!" Often depriving children of some favorite activity, privilege, or play equipment is enough to get the message through to them.

Healthy adult relationships are built on clear communication, mutual problem solving, love, and forgiveness. Our relationships with our children need those same qualities as well, even though as parents we have a unique role as we try to bring up our children.

If we say to a child, "I can forgive what you did, but I don't know if I can forget it," that's not authentic forgiveness. A child will sense that we have only buried the incident temporarily, but with a handle up for future use.

Real forgiveness is communicated by loving words and actions. Reassurances by parents at bedtime or any time can help a child realize that he or she is forgiven, loved, and accepted, and that to the best of the parent's ability, the misdeed is forgotten.

GOD LOVES US AND FORGIVES US

In family devotions, that same theme is a natural: God keeps on loving us and forgiving us even though we keep doing things that we should not do. God's love is constant and dependable, and a parent's can be, too. In fact, setting limits, teaching, and correcting our children in kind and constructive ways are rooted in that love. William and Candace Backus remind us in their book, *Empowering Parents*, "Children do have rights . . . they have the right to parental guidance, discipline, and wisdom, not the right to make all the decisions themselves."[1]

The book of James advises, "Confess your sins to one another . . . that you may be healed" (James 5:16 RSV). When family members seek both the forgiveness of God and of the person they have wronged, health-enhancing inner relief and joy will bless both children and adults with a peace that passes understanding. Too often families overlook the truth that our spiritual, physical, and mental well-being depend heavily both on our forgiving and on our being forgiven. Many authorities insist that forgiveness is one of the greatest therapeutic forces in the world.

PARENTS NEED FORGIVENESS, TOO

It is not only children who make mistakes. Every parent strikes out now and then, and sometimes we goof big-time. But how often do we readily admit our errors and say to a child, "I'm truly sorry for what I did. Will you please forgive me?" Rarely do we realize the far-reaching impact such actions have on a child. Be certain your child also hears you ask God for pardon. Witnessing genuine acts of human and divine forgiveness will have a life-changing impact on your child's future.

Many parents are not effective models for children in this regard. Wishing to appear virtuous, we sidestep admissions of wrongdoing. If we have abused a child, we have even more difficulty seeking forgiveness. Such inaction denies children the opportunity to hear us express regret and seek the child's forgiveness.

If we are mature enough to admit our weaknesses and sins, our children will be helped by our example to admit their errors and to ask God and the one(s) they've hurt for forgiveness.

CONFESSION CLEARS THE SOUL

Members of Alcoholics Anonymous do not introduce themselves by saying, "I *was* an alcoholic." They confess, "I *am* an alcoholic." In a similar way, family devotions are more helpful when parents acknowledge, "I *am* a wrongdoer" rather than "I *was* a wrongdoer." The parent who has reacted with anger toward a child should promptly ask forgiveness: "I'm sorry that I said you were selfish. Even though I felt mistreated at the time, I shouldn't have lost my cool. Will you please forgive me?" When it becomes a family pattern to promptly admit one's sins, children also will experience the joy that comes with God's promise of unconditional pardon.

THE BLESSING OF CONFESSING

"Love . . . keeps no record of wrongs."
— I Corinthians 13:5b (NIV)

In spite of good intentions, we all bungle interpersonal relationships. That could explain why one of the most frequent complaints teenagers make about parents is, "They never say 'I'm sorry' to us."

Dr. James Pennebaker sees health benefits in confessing. His interest in confessions was piqued when lie detector technicians showed him all the birthday and Christmas cards they had received from former prisoners who experienced immeasurable relief when they had an opportunity to admit their guilt.

Joan Borysenko wrote of this unusual situation:

Pennebaker recounted the story of a man who had embezzled money from the bank where he worked. He was miserable, tormented by his guilt for six months, during which time he had a steady stream of colds, bouts of the flu, and other illnesses. When he was finally called in for a lie detector test, he was naturally stressed out and anxious. But as soon as he confessed, his body went into a profound state of relaxation, even though he had entered the test a free man and completed it as a confessed embezzler who would go to jail.[2]

Sometimes confession comes unexpectedly. The following letter arrived at our high school office one October:

Attention football ticket seller . . .
Sorry, but you got cheated last Friday. I got in for $2 when it should have been $3. I knew this at the time but didn't mention it. I was wrong and want to

**confess because God won't let me get by with it. So
here's $1 that's rightfully yours.
　—A football fan**

A few weeks later we received a comparable letter in our school office:

**To whom it may concern:
You don't know me. I was a student at Franklin High
when Mr. Wright was principal. In my senior year I
cheated on my final exams. This is a letter of
apology. You see, I'm a Christian now. God has
pardoned me but I ask that you forgive me too so I
can have a clear conscience. Thank you.
　My name was Irene ＿＿＿＿＿＿＿.**

By seeking pardon soon after his offense, the football fan benefited from a clear conscience within a week. Irene's burden of repressed guilt, by contrast, had disturbed her inner peace for a third of a century because she delayed clearing her conscience. Both parents and children also penalize themselves when trying to cover up misdeeds instead of seeking pardon and peace of mind. As a result, many live with a nagging sense of alienation from God and other people.

RESENTMENT AS UNFINISHED BUSINESS

Do you carry around any bitterness against persons you have yet to forgive? If so, will your ever-alert children assume it's OK if they also cling to lingering resentments? Consider instead how your example of prompt forgiving will foster a sense of great peace and enhanced self-esteem for your precious daughter or son.

The heaviest load anyone can carry is a pack filled with enmity and grudges. Psychiatrists estimate that as many as 75 percent of those who have been deeply hurt cannot bring themselves to forgive the one who offended them. Such animosity is often an enduring saboteur of personal peace for children as well as adults.

Dr. Merle Ohlsen, a recognized authority on counseling psychology at the University of Illinois, wrote to me, "Whenever I've hurt another and fail to resolve the problem, I have some 'unfinished business.' To heal such a wrenched relationship, I must have the courage to face that person, admit my harmful act, and then request forgiveness."

SHARE THE JOY OF FORGIVENESS

God continues to forgive our sins even though we carelessly fail time after time. Yet when we accept God at his word, we're astonished by how he continues to banish our offenses to everlasting forgetfulness. The resulting peace is a gigantic step toward genuine self-esteem. When we listen to the narrations of some children, we grasp convincing illustrations of forgiveness.

In Sunday school a young girl explained, "Forgiveness is when you step on your dog's foot, but he just licks your hand." A boy in the same class shared another illustration: "Forgiveness is when you lose your dad's knife and he says, 'That's OK, it was rusty anyway.' "

Since God accepts each of us as we are, how can we fail to accept our children as they were created?

INSIGHTS FOR PARENTS

1. Unforgiven wrongs lodge in hidden recesses of our minds. Often such offenses persistently but needlessly disrupt a parent's or a child's inner peace.

2. "Humanity is never so beautiful as when praying for forgiveness or forgiving another." —Jean Paul Richter

3. "Everyone claims that forgiveness is a wonderful idea, until they have something to forgive." —C. S. Lewis

4. "A Christian will find it much cheaper to pardon than to resent. Forgiveness saves the expense of anger, the cost of hatred, and the waste of energy."—Hannah Moore

5. Forgiveness, like dimming our headlights in courtesy to other drivers, happens sooner when we take the initiative. Slow forgiveness is little better than no forgiveness.

6. "Be . . . tender-hearted, forgiving one another as God in Christ forgave you."—Ephesians 4:32 (NEB)

7. Forgiving others fosters health. Resentments are poisonous and serve to diminish the unforgiving self.

8. A helpful prayer: "Help us, Lord, to view the faults of every individual in our family through the eyes of divine forgiveness."

9. "Forgive us the wrong we have done, as we have forgiven those who have wronged us."—Matthew 6:12 (NEB)

10. "All have sinned and are far away from God's saving presence. But by the free gift of God's grace they are all put right with him through Jesus Christ, who sets them free."—Romans 3:23 (TEV)

THINGS TO DO

A. Confessing personal faults never has been a favorite human venture, so this may be a difficult challenge. Yet the resulting mercy, freedom, joy, and love make the effort most worthwhile. Be honest with yourself. On a piece of paper, write a response to this question: "How common is it for me to rationalize my action after inflicting hurt on another person?" Any examples you write about can be used in step B.

B. As an individual or as a member of a parent group, title a sheet of paper "Unfinished Business." Identify people whose forgiveness you need. Select one and pray for God's guidance. Next, contact that individual by person, by phone, or by letter. Confess your resentment or other wrongdoing and seek his or her pardon. Also accept God's forgiveness. Finally, obliterate that entry from your "unfinished business" list.

As you experience release from the burden, thank God for your new peace, joy, and freedom. With new confidence, choose another name on your list and repeat the process of reconciliation. Relish each experience of liberating peace.

C. At an appropriate time, share such an experience with a child facing a similar difficult challenge and needing forgiveness. Offer the encouragement of your personal release after choosing between continual grudge-clutching and seeking God's help to triumph over the distressing burden of "unfinished business."

14

God-Sponsored Self-Worth

God loves each of us as if there were only one of us.

—Augustine

One Sunday when our pastor announced that it was time for his message to children in the congregation, most of the youngsters scampered to the front and plopped down around him. The shy ones inched their way forward cautiously, still clutching a parent's hand, but all eyes were on Pastor Dan as he knelt to tell the children a story.

His first words quickened their curiosity. Looking to the back of the sanctuary, he called out, "Here, Pal." A dog raced down the aisle and into his arms. Pastor Dan explained to the excited children that he'd trained the family dog to obey various spoken commands. To the delight of each child, Pal obeyed the pastor's instructions to "Sit," "Speak," "Shake hands," and "Roll over." After each trick, Pastor Dan rewarded Pal with a tasty treat.

PERFORMANCE-BASED LOVE

Pal had to work for each of his rewards. By pleasing his master, he earned words of encouragement, a treat to eat, and a pat on the head. Many of us in church, like Pal, think we need to act in acceptable ways to earn God's love. It's so easy to overlook God's promise that a sense of authentic self-worth is free, a gracious gift from a loving heavenly Father.

It's my prayer that moms and dads reading this book will free each child from the burden of earning a sense of self-worth by conforming to some parent-pleasing standards. In our competitive society it's difficult to realize that we are accepted by

God not because of our achievements but because of God's un-restricted love.

FAUCET LOVE

We probably never said to a child, "I'll give you food if you do as I say, if you measure up to my wishes." Yet many children do hear, "How can I love you when you continually embarrass me with your behavior?" And perhaps some parents have said, "If you can't bring home top grades, you'll never see Disneyland!"

Provisional love is either doled out or denied by an authority figure. A father, for example, may withhold his love for a child who fails to follow his mandate. This is "faucet love." In effect, this dad is saying, "You'll qualify for my love if you do exactly as I say. When you fail to conform, the love faucet is turned off!"

Consider how some parents today might welcome home a prodigal son. When the nomadic drifter is still some distance from home, the father recognizes his wandering son but locks the front door. He lets his spendthrift son ring the doorbell several times before he answers.

Finally, the father opens the door and directs, "Sit down over there and we'll discuss what you've done." A long lecture follows, ending with, "I hope you're ashamed of how you've dragged our family's reputation in the mud. Go to your room. Tomorrow I'll spell out the conditions you have to meet in order for you to stay here or to be considered part of the family."

This approach is the reverse of our heavenly Father's un-restricted love for you and for me—God's model for our parental relationship with each of our children.

LIKE PARENTS, LIKE KIDS

"love does not keep a record of wrongs . . ."
—I Corinthians 13:5 (TEV)

In spite of our best efforts, every parent will bungle some family relationships. Isn't it foolish, then, for us to hope for flawless children? Instead, we should offer them a proven technique for reconciliation after each of our mistakes when we confess, "I'm sorry! Please forgive me for what I said (or did)." Examples of genuine confession have a greater impact than all our words encouraging our children to ask for forgiveness.

LOVE WITH NO PRECONDITIONS

God's love is a paradox to the human mind. Our society considers it poor business to give without gaining something in return, yet God pleads with us, "How long will you misunderstand my plan of salvation? I've never insisted that you do what is impossible—become faultless because you think then you will qualify for my love. Your value to me never depends on your accomplishments. My love is never fickle. You can count on it today and every day. It never wavers, never fails."

NO "HOPELESS BLUNDERS"

Phillip Brooks claimed that it's common for youth to conclude, "I'm inadequate, worthless, a no-good." Reflecting on God's gracious forgiveness, however, Brooks concludes, "God makes no hopeless blunders."

Abbe Henri De Tourville came to a similar conclusion about God's generous, though unwarranted, love. He suggests that each day we acknowledge, "I am loved by God more than I can ever conceive or understand." De Tourville wisely adds that, because that is true, parents should help each child comprehend "the wonderful thought that God loves you with a tenderness, a generosity, and an intimacy which surpass all your dreams."[1]

Parents who wish to serve as positive models for their children need to accept God at his word. "When anyone is joined to Christ, he [or she] is a new being. . . . All this is done by God" (2 Corinthians 5:17-18, TEV).

A CHILD OF GOD

My friend Carlos told me one day about his long struggles for self-worth and his eventual growth.

"At last I realized that claiming the full meaning of my baptism was basic to my positive self-concept," he said. "For years

I'd overlooked that I was already a child of God. I can't remember my baptism, but when its true significance struck me, that event early in life became the cornerstone of my sense of worth. I understood that as a baby there was no way I could have earned God's love. Yet at that early moment God accepted me with zero personal qualifications. I see how foolish I've been all these years, striving for a worthiness on my own. Now, my whole life has taken on a triumphant new meaning."

God's unlimited love and acceptance of us at our baptism, whether we were baptized when we were babies or as adults, is awe-inspiring. For those of us in churches that baptize infants, parents can help each child comprehend the blessing of being a beloved child of God by celebrating the child's baptismal anniversary. Sunday school leaders could also consider commemorating each child's baptismal birthday.

PARENTS ARE FORGIVEN TOO

Many childhood influences are beyond the control of parents. A child's temperament, as well as environmental forces like peer influence, are examples of pressures that can be beyond a parent's control. As a result, conscientious moms and dads may suffer serious doubts, even guilt, about their child-rearing abilities. Even though we fumble while trying to do our best, it's helpful to confess our humanness both to our children and to God. Fortunately, God is a major-league forgiver of both parents and children. That's good news for us all!

GOD'S "NOBODIES"

Leo Bustad, dean emeritus of veterinary medicine at Washington State University, frequently speaks to the needs of parents and children at the Holden Village retreat center in central Washington. Bustad emphasizes that while many of us may feel we're only a small cog in a big machine, God looks on every child and adult as a person of infinite value and great potential. Each of us can accept the fact that we are a child of God, at times rebellious and wayward, yet still God's beloved daughter or son.

God doesn't choose just superstars or prodigies to do his work. He typically appoints ordinary people like us with built-in flaws to handle his tasks. Remember how Moses felt when God asked him to help? He also focused on his inadequacies: "Just look around a little more, God. I'm sure you'll find someone else much more qualified for this responsibility."

Consider the disciples whom our Lord selected to share the good news. Most were plain, commonplace, everyday individuals. Also recall that Jesus went out of his way to talk with the insignificant and neglected, the "nobodies" of that day. He sought out and befriended children, tax collectors, prostitutes, beggars, blind people, lepers, and the deaf. He ate and drank with some people many of us might not invite into our homes—or into our church.

Bustad directs our attention to some of the so-called nonentities in Jesus' world. He relates there was a day when children were swarming around and the disciples were trying to run them off—to keep the kids with the runny noses and sticky fingers off Jesus' back. But Jesus restrained the disciples. He welcomed the children—runny noses and all—and went on to tell his disciples, "of such is the Kingdom of Heaven" . . . it wouldn't be heaven without them.

Reflecting on these events, Bustad says we are forced to accept that there could be absolutely no one—no matter how young or old, how crippled or deformed, how retarded, how lonely or rejected, how inconsequential—who could possibly be forgotten or neglected by our loving heavenly Father. And that's what Jesus came to disclose—his kind of world where no one is forgotten . . . where there are no Miss Nobodies . . . no Mrs. Nobodies . . . no Mr. Nobodies.

Until we parents and our children can accept and love ourselves as God created us, we will have insufficient love to share with others. If we perceive ourselves as unworthy of God's love, we will continue to be emotionally deprived, handicapped in both giving and receiving love.

Yet God has underwritten the self-worth of each of us and of every child. Thank God there is no question but that all in your family are individuals of genuine worth where it really counts— in the eyes of their heavenly Father.

1. God doesn't love each of us because we're worthwhile; we're worthwhile because God loves us.

2. Since there are no perfect human beings, we can never expect to become perfect parents, though with God's love and guidance each of us keeps learning.

3. Paul speaks directly to parents when he says, "Love is patient and kind. . . . Love does not keep a record of wrongs" (1 Corinthians 13:4 TEV).

4. Unconditional love has no strings attached. Children should never feel they must match or exceed the accomplishments of another.

5. We should refuse to waste time looking in life's rearview mirror, tormenting ourselves with past events we can't change. Instead, let us pray daily for God's help to become accepting, compassionate, loving parents to our young people.

6. God sees each of us as we can be but still loves us as we are.

7. Supreme happiness in each child's life results from the conviction that they are fully accepted by their earthly parents and their heavenly Father.

8. Parents affect eternity. We can never know where our influence will stop.

| THINGS TO DO |

A. With other parents or with your spouse, identify five qualities you hope your children someday will select when describing their childhood relationship with you. After each quality, specify at least one parenting practice you believe will reinforce that quality in your child's memory.

B. Place each family member's name and baptismal anniversary date on your home calendar. Discuss with other parents or with your spouse how a family might commemorate such important events with appropriate reminders of God's wonderful gift of unconditional acceptance and love. Consider similar recognitions on the baptismal anniversary of any child for whom you've been a godparent.

15

The Master Key to Self-Esteem

Love is the medicine for the sickness of mankind. We can live if we have love.

—Karl Menninger

Every girl and boy needs an abundance of love—unrestricted, freely given love—in the home. Children should not suffer the distress of feeling unwanted by the very persons who brought them into the world. Lifelong disabling of a child's self-worth can occur in the home, a place that should be a safe haven and loving shelter.

Today experts agree that love is the key to therapeutic programs in modern psychiatric hospitals. Love, then, must also be the key to positive parent-child relationships in today's family. By contrast, children who experience little or no love at home find their lives emotionally and spiritually bleak. Such youngsters are not responsible for the painful, abusive environment into which they were born. Unfortunately, children convinced that their moms and dads don't love them somehow feel responsible for their parents' rejection. The child thinks, "Something must be wrong with me if they can't love me!"

ACCEPTING VERSUS CHERISHING

Sometimes we hear child specialists encouraging parents to accept their children. This sounds like constructive advice, but it's inadequate to meet a child's needs. "Accepting" may amount to little more than tolerating a youngster. Children need to be convinced that they're cherished by the most important persons in the world to them: Mom and Dad. This will assure them that

their homes remain a secure refuge of love where each child learns to accept himself and also other people.

TO BE PARENTS LIKE GOD THE FATHER

Children have a deep hunger to hear that they're loved by their mother and father. For a variety of reasons, a certain stiffness or awkwardness may restrain a dad from voicing his love for a child. Moms usually do not have as much difficulty. Such restraint often is more pronounced in father-son relationships than in others. A dad should never assume that a child *knows* of his love. Both daughters and sons long to actually *hear* both parents express their affection with the simple statement, "I love you."

As previously suggested, an earthly father's indifferent and distant relationship with a child can block that child's accepting and loving relationship with a heavenly Father.

COMMUNICATE YOUR LOVE

If children are uncomfortable with a display of affection, parents can develop a secret code of caring known only in that family. For example, some children know in advance that when a parent squeezes their hand or shoulder the parent is telling them, "I love you!"[1] Variations of this approach could be particularly helpful for fathers and sons, although mothers and daughters are often just as needy and just as blessed by these love signals.

Families may claim that love is the foundation of their home, yet many children find it a silent love, one that is either under-expressed or unexpressed. This failure is often a major contributor to extended grieving when death occurs in a family. Survivors anguish over what they wish they had shared—expressions of their silent love they'll never be able to communicate. Declare your love and affection to those dear to you while there is still time.

CHERISHING OTHER CHILDREN

One of the most rewarding decisions you can make is to help repair the damaged self-images of other youngsters in your neighborhood or church. You'll love it. While the idea may sound improbable, you may be the only model of God's caring love that some youth will experience.

Every community has numerous hurting youth who are "different," who are convinced they're friendless—the unlovely in appearance, the small child, the fat child, the slow learner, the minority, or the handicapped child. At the same time, innumerable youth appear on the surface to have their lives together but their self-esteem is in shambles.

A few words of support and encouragement from nonfamily adults had a lasting impact on me as a kid. I'll never forget the positive influence of caring men and women like my junior choir director at church, my positive aunt who regularly expressed appreciation when I mowed the lawn, and my confidence-boosting high school physics teacher without whose inspiration I would not have enrolled in college. At other times, a few adult friends simply said they were upholding me in their prayers at particularly stressful times. Not one of them had anything to gain by their supportive concern for a young person filled with self-doubts. Yet without such caring support of loving adults, the lives of innumerable youth might lack personal fulfillment or social usefulness.

MISSION FIELDS RIGHT AT HOME

Divisive pressures on families are tearing many communities apart. Increasing numbers of neglected children are roaming free, joining gangs, shooting enemies, and looking desperately for love. As a result, each Christian believer lives in the midst of a local mission field with enormous needs.

Our first priority must be to maintain substantial love-bank balances for each of our children. Next, we should be alert to the self-esteem needs of emotionally bruised children in our neighborhoods and congregations. We can function as emissaries of God's love right where we live. Our informal ministry to youth who feel inadequate can lift their sagging self-esteem, not just for today but for a lifetime. Youngsters we help now may someday look back and thank God for our support when they most needed an adult's interest, confidence, and cherishing love.

What a tremendous opportunity each of us has to be a positive influence on tomorrow's world by giving of our time and God's love to nourish the self-worth of children and youth in our homes and in our communities. Dwell each day on the Apostle Paul's suggestion to "fill your mind with those things that are good and deserve praise: things that are true, noble, right, pure, lovely and honorable" (Phil. 4:8, TEV).

You will help change our world—for the better.

INSIGHTS FOR PARENTS

I. Life's genuine joy for children is to know they are loved by the most important persons in the world to them—their mom and dad.

2. "Love is patient and kind. . . . Love never ends. . . ."—1 Corinthians 13:4-8 (RSV)

3. God's love cannot be earned, but it can be spurned. What do your children learn from watching your response to God's love?

4. Accept God's gracious gift of unequivocal love for you. Then share his limitless love with each child in your home as well as with love-starved children in your local "mission field."

5. Those who seem to deserve love the least, often need it the most.

6. "How great is the love the Father has lavished on us, that we should be called children of God! And that is what we are!"—1 John 3:1 (NIV)

7. "If we could raise one generation of children with un-conditional love, there would be no more Hitlers."—Elisabeth Kübler-Ross

8. Each child's sense of self-worth is influenced not only by those who love the child, but—more than we realize—by those unable to love the child.

9. "This is my commandment, that you love one another as I have loved you."—John 15:12

10. "The supreme happiness in life is the conviction that we are loved."—Victor Hugo

---

THINGS TO DO

A. Ask your children's friends what their favorite experiences are (1) as a family, (2) with their mother, or (3) with their father. Draw on their responses to evaluate your own parent-child activities and to plan future experiences that family members may treasure for years to come. Share the summary lists with other interested parents.

B. From your own observations and from talking with others, find out who some of the children and teenagers are in your community or congregation who would enjoy friendships with your family. Think about what you or other families might do to help them feel better about themselves.

FURTHER READING

Backus, William, and Candace Backus.
Empowering Parents, How to Raise Obedient Children—It's Possible, It's Right. Minneapolis: Bethany House, 1992.

Borysenko, Joan.
Guilt Is the Teacher, Love Is the Lesson. New York: Warner Books, 1990.

Briggs, Dorothy Corkille.
Your Child's Self-Esteem: The Key to Life. Garden City, NY: Dolphin Books, 1975.

Clarke, Jean Illsley.
Self-Esteem: A Family Affair. New York: Harper & Row, 1978.

Dobson, James.
Hide or Seek. Old Tappen, NJ: Fleming H. Revell Company, 1979.

Drakeford, John W.
The Awesome Power of the Listening Heart. Grand Rapids, MI: Zondervan Publishing House, 1982.

Erickson, Kenneth.
The Power of Praise. St. Louis, MO: Concordia Publishing House, 1984.

Forward, Susan.
Toxic Parents: Overcoming Their Hurtful Legacy and Reclaiming Your Life. New York: Bantam Books, 1989.

Grant, Wilson Wayne, M.D.
The Power of Affirming Touch. Minneapolis: Augsburg Publishing House, 1986.

Smalley, Gary, and John Trent, Ph.D.
The Blessing. Nashville, TN: Thomas Nelson Publishers, 1986.

Tournier, Paul.
The Meaning of Persons. New York: Harper & Row, 1957.

ENDNOTES

Preface

1. James Dobson, *Hide or Seek* (Old Tappan, NJ: Fleming H. Revell Co., 1974), 20, 21.

2. *Effective Christian Education: A National Study of Protestant Denominations* (Minneapolis: Search Institute, 1990).

Chapter 1/Where Self-Esteem Begins

1. Paul Tournier, *Escape from Loneliness* (Philadelphia: Westminster Press, 1962), 17.

Chapter 2/What We Do Has Lasting Effects

1. Susan Forward, *Toxic Parents* (New York: Bantam Books, 1989), 4.

2. James Dobson, *Hide or Seek* (Old Tappan, NJ: Fleming H. Revell Co., 1974), 20.

Chapter 3/When Children Are Belittled and Discounted

1. John Gardiner, from *Daily Guideposts*, 7th ed. (Carmel, N.Y. 1983), 289.

2. Linda Mouat, "Shadow Brother," *Christian Parenting Today*, September/October 1991, 49–50.

3. Skipper McCaghy, and Lafton McCaghy, *In Their Own Behalf* (New York: Appleton-Century-Crofts, 1968), 200.

4. James Dobson, *Hide or Seek* (Old Tappan, NJ: Fleming H. Revell Co., 1974), 90.

Chapter 5/Practicing Good Communication

1. RespecTeen, "Straight to Parents" (Minneapolis: Padilla Speer Beardsley, Inc., June 6, 1991).

2. Joan Borysenko, *Guilt Is the Teacher, Love Is the Lesson* (New York: Warner Books, 1990), 71.

Chapter 7/When There Are Wounds

1. Joan Borysenko, *Guilt Is the Teacher, Love Is the Lesson* (New York: Warner Books, 1990), 70.

2. "Girls Who Go Too Far," *Newsweek*, July 22, 1991, 58.

Chapter 8/How Put-Downs Harm Children

1. A story from the Associated Press in Medford, Oreg., the *Register Guard*, March 1, 1990, 3B.
2. Susan Forward, *Toxic Parents* (New York: Bantam Books, 1989), 98.
3. Thomas Gordon, *Parent Effectiveness Training* (New York: Peter H. Wyden, Inc., 1970), 31–32.

Chapter 9/Nurturing Family Members

1. Thomas Gordon, *Parent Effectiveness Training* (New York: Peter H. Wyden, Inc., 1970), chap. 13.
2. James Davidson Hunter and Lou Harris Associates, Inc. *The Girl Scouts Survey on the Beliefs and Moral Values of America's Children* (1989). Available from Girl Scouts Headquarters in New York, N.Y.

Chapter 10/Different Gifts, All Accepted

1. Paul Tournier, *The Strong and the Weak* (Philadelphia: Westminster Press, 1963), 57.
2. Used by permission.

Chapter 11/Trying to Earn Acceptance and Love

1. Bob Derr, "Shepherd of the Truck Stops," *The Lutheran*, September 1987, 10.
2. Edward F. Markquart, from "In His Father's Arms," *The Lutheran*, February 14, 1990, 11.
3. Mike Yorkey, *Growing a Healthy Home* (Brentwood, Tenn.: Wolgemuth and Hyatt Publishers, 1990), 189.

Chapter 12/The Power of Touch

1. "Kangaroo Care and Preemies," *Reader's Digest*, December 1992, 255. Original source: Elisabeth Rosenthal in *The New York Times*.
2. "Meet: Will Hayes," *NEA Today*, December 1987, 11.
3. Gary Smalley and John Trent, *Home Remedies* (Portland, Oreg.: Multnomah Press, 1991), 178.

Chapter 13/The Need for Forgiveness

1. William Backus and Candace Backus, *Empowering Parents* (Minneapolis: Bethany House, 1992), 24.

2. Joan Borysenko, *Guilt Is the Teacher, Love Is the Lesson* (New York: Warner Books, 1990), 179.

Chapter 14/God-Sponsored Self-Worth

1. Abbe Henri De Tourville, *Letters of Direction* (Ridgefield, Conn.: Morehouse Publishing Co., 1939), 78.

Chapter 15/The Master Key to Self-Esteem

1. Ralph Kinney Bennett, "What Kids Most Need in a Dad," *Reader's Digest*, February 1992, 92.